HOW
TO
MEDITATE

HOW
TO
MEDITATE

A PRACTICAL GUIDE TO MAKING
FRIENDS WITH YOUR MIND

PEMA CHÖDRÖN

sounds true
BOULDER, COLORADO

Sounds True, Inc.
Boulder, CO 80306

Copyright © 2013 Pema Chödrön

Sounds True is a trademark of Sounds True, Inc.

Gotsampa's "Seven Delights" on page 146 was translated under the guidance of Khenpo Tsultrim Gyamtso Rinpoche by Jim Scott in collaboration with Anne Buchardi, Karmê Choling, Barnet, Vermont, August, 1996. Reprinted with permission from the translator.

Published 2013

Cover and book design by Rachael Murray

Cover photo © Sandy MacKenzie from Shutterstock.com

Printed in the United States of America

  Library of Congress Cataloging-in-Publication Data
Chödrön, Pema.
  How to meditate : a practical guide to making friends with your mind /
Pema Chödrön.
    pages cm
  ISBN 978-1-60407-933-3
  1. Meditation--Buddhism. I. Title.
  BQ5612.C48 2013
  294.3'4435--dc23
                                    2012046126

Ebook ISBN: 978-1-62203-048-4

10 9 8 7 6 5 4 3 2 1

*Meditation is simply training our state of being
so that our mind and body can be synchronized.
Through the practice of meditation, we can learn to be
without deception, to be fully genuine and alive.*
—CHÖGYAM TRUNGPA RINPOCHE

*Our life is an endless journey: the practice of meditation
allows us to experience all the textures of the roadway,
which is what the journey is all about.*
—CHÖGYAM TRUNGPA RINPOCHE

CONTENTS

Choosing to Live Wholeheartedly

The principle of nowness is very important to any effort to establish an enlightened society. You may wonder what the best approach is to helping society and how you can know that what you are doing is authentic and good. The only answer is nowness. The way to relax, or rest the mind in nowness, is through the practice of meditation. In meditation you take an unbiased approach. You let things be as they are, without judgment, and in that way you yourself learn to be.

—CHÖGYAM TRUNGPA RINPOCHE

The mind is very wild. The human experience is full of unpredictability and paradox, joys and sorrows, successes and failures. We can't escape any of these experiences in the vast terrain of our existence. It is part of what makes life grand—and it is also why our minds take us on such a crazy ride. If we can train ourselves through meditation to be more open and more accepting toward the wild arc of our experience, if we can lean into the difficulties of life and the ride of our minds, we can become more settled and relaxed amid whatever life brings us.

There are numerous ways to work with the mind. One of the most effective ways is through the tool of sitting meditation. Sitting meditation opens us to each and every moment of our life. Each moment is totally unique and unknown. Our mental world is seemingly predictable and graspable. We believe that thinking through all the events and to-dos of our life will provide us with ground and security. But it's all a fantasy, and this very moment, free of conceptual overlay, is completely unique. It is absolutely unknown. We've never experienced this very moment before, and the next moment will not be the same as the one we are in now. Meditation teaches us how to relate to life directly, so that we can truly experience the present moment, free from conceptual overlay.

If we look at the dharma—in other words, the teachings of the Buddha, the truth of what is—we see that through the practice of meditation the intention is to remove suffering. Maybe that's why so many people are attracted to meditation, because generally people don't find themselves sitting in the meditation posture unless they have something that's bothering them. But the Buddhist teachings are not only about removing the symptoms of suffering, they're about actually removing the cause, or the root, of suffering. The Buddha said, "I teach only one thing: suffering and the cessation of suffering."

In this book, I want to emphasize that the root of suffering is mind—our minds. And also, the root of happiness is our mind. The sage Shantideva, in the *Bodhicaryavatara,* in talking about the subject of suffering, offered a famous analogy for how we try to alleviate our suffering. He's said that if you walk on the earth and it's hurting your feet, you might want to cover all the earth with hides of leather, so that you'd never have to suffer from the pain of the ground. But where could such an amount of leather be found? Rather, you could simply wrap a bit of leather around your feet, and then it's as if the whole world is covered with leather and you're always protected.

In other words, you could endlessly try to have suffering cease by dealing with outer circumstances—and that's usually what all of us do. It is the usual approach; you just try to solve the outer problem again and again and again. But the Buddha said something quite revolutionary, which most of us don't really buy: if you work with your mind, you will alleviate all the suffering that seems to come from the outside. When something is bothering you—a person is bugging you, a situation is irritating you, or physical pain is troubling you—you must work with your mind, and that is done through meditation. Working with our minds is the only means through which we'll actually begin to feel happy and contented with the world that we live in.

There's an important distinction that needs to be made about the word "suffering." When the Buddha said, "The only thing I teach is suffering and the cessation of suffering," he used the word *dukkha* for suffering. Dukkha is different than pain. Pain is an inevitable part of human life, as is pleasure. Pain and pleasure alternate, and they're just part and parcel of anybody who has a body and a mind and is born into this world.

The Buddha didn't say that, "I teach only one thing: pain and the cessation of pain." He said pain *is*—you have to grow up to the fact, mature to the fact, relax to the fact that there will be pain in your life. You're not going to reach the point where, if someone you love dies, you won't feel grief. You're not going to reach the point where if you fall down a flight of stairs you're not bruised. As you age, your back might hurt and your knees might ache. These things and many others could happen.

Even the most advanced meditator has moods. The quality of energy moving through people—the heavier, more oppressive energies that we call depression, or fear, or anxiety—these kinds of mood energies run through all beings, just as the weather changes from day to day. Our internal weather is shifting and changing all the time, whether we're fully enlightened or not. The question then becomes, how do we work with these shifting energies? Do we need to completely identify with them and get carried away and dragged down by them?

The word *dukkha* is also translated as "dissatisfaction," or "never satisfied." Dukkha is kept alive by being continually dissatisfied with the reality of the human condition, which means being continually dissatisfied with the fact that pleasant and unpleasant situations are part and parcel of life. There's a strong tendency on the part of all living beings to want the pleasant, agreeable, comfortable, secure feelings to be all-pervasive. If there's pain in any form—if there's anything disagreeable, uncomfortable, or insecure—we want to run away from that and avoid it. This is why we turn to meditation.

WHY MEDITATE?

We do not meditate in order to be comfortable. In other words, we don't meditate in order to always, all the time, feel good. I imagine shockwaves are passing through you as you read this, because so many people come to meditation to simply "feel better." However, the purpose of meditation is not to feel bad, you'll be glad to know. Rather, meditation gives us the opportunity to have an open, compassionate attentiveness to whatever is going on. The meditative space is like the big sky—spacious, vast enough to accommodate anything that arises.

In meditation, our thoughts and emotions can become like clouds that dwell and pass away. Good and comfortable, pleasing and difficult and painful—all of this comes and goes. So the essence of meditation is training in something that is quite radical and definitely not the habitual pattern of the species: And that is to stay with ourselves no matter what is happening, without putting labels of good and bad, right and wrong, pure and impure, on top of our experience.

If meditation was just about feeling good (and I think all of us secretly hope that is what it's about), we would often feel like we must be doing it wrong. Because at times, meditation can be such a difficult experience. A very common experience of the meditator, in a typical day or on a typical retreat, is the experience of boredom, restlessness, a hurting back, pain in the knees—even the mind might be hurting—so many "not feeling good" experiences. Instead, meditation is about a compassionate openness and the ability to be with oneself and one's situation through all kinds of experiences. In meditation, you're open to whatever life presents you with. It's about touching the earth and coming back to being right here. While some kinds of meditation are more about achieving special states and somehow transcending or rising above the difficulties of life, the kind of meditation that I've trained in and that I am teaching here is about awakening fully to our life. It's about opening the heart and mind to the difficulties and the joys of life—just as it is. And the fruits of this kind of meditation are boundless.

As we meditate, we are nurturing five qualities that begin to come forth over the months and years that we practice. You might find it helpful to reconnect with these qualities whenever you ask yourself, "Why am I meditating?" The first quality—namely, the first thing that we're doing when we meditate—is cultivating and nurturing steadfastness with ourselves. I was talking to someone about this once, and she asked, "Is this steadfastness sort of like loyalty? What are we being loyal to?" Through meditation, we are developing a loyalty to ourselves. This steadfastness that we cultivate in meditation translates immediately into loyalty to one's experience of life.

Steadfastness means that when you sit down to meditate and you allow yourself to experience what's happening in that moment—which could be your mind going a hundred miles an hour, your body twitching, your head pounding, your heart full of fear, whatever comes up—you stay with the experience. That's it. Sometimes you can sit there for an hour and it doesn't get any better. Then you might say, "Bad meditation session. I just had a bad meditation session." But the willingness to sit there for ten minutes, fifteen minutes, twenty minutes, a half hour, an hour, however long you sat there—this is a compassionate gesture of developing loyalty or steadfastness to yourself.

We have such a tendency to lay a lot of labels, opinions, and judgments on top of what's happening. Steadfastness—loyalty to yourself—means that you let those judgments go. So, in a way, part of the steadfastness is that when you notice your mind is going a million miles an hour and you're thinking about all kinds of things, there is this uncontrived moment that just happens without any effort: you stay with your experience.

In meditation, you develop this nurturing quality of loyalty and steadfastness and perseverance toward yourself. And as we learn to do this in meditation, we become more able to persevere through all kinds of situations outside of our meditation, or what we call postmeditation.

The second quality that we generate in meditation is clear seeing, which is similar to steadfastness. Sometimes this is called clear awareness. Through meditation, we develop the ability to catch ourselves when we are spinning off, or hardening to circumstances and people, or somehow closing down to life. We start to catch the beginnings of a neurotic chain reaction that limits our ability to experience joy or connect with others. You would think that because we are sitting in meditation, so quiet and still, focusing on the breath, that we wouldn't notice very much. But it is actually quite the opposite. Through this development of steadfastness, this learning to stay in meditation, we begin to form a nonjudgmental, unbiased clarity of just seeing. Thoughts come, emotions come, and we can see them ever so clearly.

In meditation, you are moving closer and closer to yourself, and you begin to understand yourself so much more clearly. You begin to see clearly without a conceptual analysis, because with regular practice, you see what you do over and over and over and over again. You see that you replay the same tapes over and over and over in your mind. The name of the partner might be different, the employer might be different, but the themes are somewhat repetitious. Meditation helps us to clearly see ourselves and the habitual patterns that limit our life. You begin to see your opinions clearly. You see your judgments. You see your defense mechanisms. Meditation deepens your understanding of yourself.

The third quality we cultivate in meditation is one that I've actually been alluding to when I bring up both steadfastness and clear seeing—and it happens when we allow ourselves to sit in meditation with our emotional distress. I think it's really important to state this as a separate quality that we develop in practice, because when we experience emotional distress in meditation (and we will), we often feel like "we're doing it wrong." So the third quality that seems to organically develop within us is the cultivation of courage, the gradual arising of courage. I think the word "gradual" here is very important, because it can be a slow process. But over time, you will find yourself developing the courage to experience your emotional discomfort, and the trials and tribulations of life.

Meditation is a transformative process, rather than a magic makeover in which we doggedly aim to change something about ourselves. The more we practice, the more we open, and the more we develop courage in our life. In meditation you never really feel that you "did it" or that you've "arrived." You feel that you just relaxed enough to experience what's always been within you. I sometimes call this transformative process "grace." Because when we're developing this courage, in which we allow the range of our emotions to occur, we can be struck with moments of insight, insights that could never have come from trying to figure out conceptually what's wrong with us, or what's wrong with the world. These moments of insight come from the act of sitting in meditation, which takes courage, a courage that grows with time.

Through this developing courage, we are often graced with a change in our worldview, if ever so slight. Meditation allows you to see something fresh that you've never seen before or to understand something new that you've never understood before. Sometimes we call these boons of meditation "blessings." In meditation, you learn how to get out of your own way long enough for there to be room for your own wisdom to manifest, and this happens because you're not repressing this wisdom any longer.

When you develop the courage to experience your emotional distress at its most difficult level, and you're just sitting there with it in meditation, you realize how much comfort and how much security you get from your mental world. Because, at that point, when there's a lot of emotion, you begin to really get in touch with the feeling, the underlying energy, of your emotions. As you will learn in this book, you begin to let go of the words, the stories, as best you can, and then you're just sitting there. Then you realize, even if it seems unpleasant, that you feel compelled to keep reliving the memory, the story of your emotions—or that you want to dissociate. You may find that you often drift into fantasy about something pleasant. And the secret is that, actually, we don't want to do any of this. Part of us wants so earnestly to wake up and open. The human species wants to feel more alive and awake to life. But also, the human species is not comfortable with the transient, shifting quality of the energy of reality. Simply put, a large part of us actually prefers the comfort of our mental fantasies and planning, and that's actually why this practice is so difficult to do. Experiencing our emotional distress and nurturing all of these qualities—steadfastness, clear seeing, courage—really shakes up our habitual patterns. Meditation loosens up our conditioning; it's loosening up the way we hold ourselves together, the way that we perpetuate our suffering.

The fourth quality we develop in meditation is something I've been touching on all along, and that is the ability to become awake to our lives, to each and every moment, just as it is. This is the absolute essence of meditation. We develop attention to this very moment; we learn to just be here. And we have a lot of resistance to just being here! When I first started practicing, I thought I wasn't good at it. It took me a while to realize that I had a lot of resistance to just being here now. Just being here—attention to this very moment—does not provide us with any kind of certainty or predictability. But when we learn how to relax into the present moment, we learn how to relax with the unknown.

Life is never predictable. You can say, "Oh, I like the unpredictability," but that's usually true only up to a certain point, as long as the unpredictability is somewhat fun and adventurous. I have a lot of relatives who are into things like bungee-jumping and all kinds of terrifying things—all my nephews, particularly, and nieces. Sometimes, thinking of their activities, I experience extreme terror. But everybody, even my wild relatives, meets their edge. And sometimes the most adventurous of us meet our edge in the strangest places, like when we can't get a good cup of coffee. We're willing to jump off a bridge upside down, but we throw a tantrum when we can't get a good cup of coffee. Strange that not being able to get a good cup of coffee could be the unknown, but somehow for some, maybe for you, it is that edge of stepping into that uncomfortable, uncertain space.

So this place of meeting our edge, of accepting the present moment and the unknown, is a very powerful place for the person who wishes to awaken and open their heart and mind. The present moment is the generative fire of our meditation. It is what propels us toward transformation. In other words, the present moment is the fuel for your personal journey. Meditation helps you to meet your edge; it's where you actually come up against it and you start to lose it. Meeting the unknown of the moment allows you to live your life and to enter your relationships and commitments ever more fully. This is living wholeheartedly.

Meditation is revolutionary, because it's not a final resting place: you can be much, much more settled. This is why I continue to do this year after year. If I looked back and had no sense that any transformation had happened, if I didn't recognize that I feel more settled and more flexible, it would be pretty discouraging. But there is that feeling. And there's always another challenge, and that keeps us humble. Life knocks you off your pedestal. We can always work on meeting the unknown from a more settled and openhearted space. It happens for all of us. You think that you have it all together and that you're really chilled out, and then something really blows it for you. For example, here you are beginning to read a book on how to meditate from "a settled nun." And you need to know that things happen that cause me to become like a little brat. I too have moments where I am challenged in meeting the present moment, even after years of meditation. Years back, I took a trip alone with my granddaughter, who was six years old at the time. It was such an embarrassing experience, because she was being extremely difficult. She was saying "no" about everything, and I just kept losing it with this little angel whom I just adore. So I said, "OK, Alexandria, this is between you and Grandma, right? You're not going to tell anybody about what's going on? You know, all those pictures you've seen of Grandma on the front of books? Anyone you see carrying around one of those books, you do not tell them about this!"

The point is that when your cover is blown, it's embarrassing. When you practice meditation, getting your cover blown is just as embarrassing as it ever was, but you're glad to see where you're still stuck because you would like to die with no more big surprises. On your deathbed, when you thought you were St. Whoever, you don't want to find out that the nurse completely pushes you over the wall with frustration and anger. Not only do you die angry at the nurse, but you die disillusioned with your whole being. So if you ask why we meditate,

I would say it's so we can become more flexible and tolerant to the present moment. You could be irritated with the nurse when you're dying and say, "You know, that's the way life is." You let it move through you. You can feel settled with that, and hopefully you even die laughing—it was just your luck to get this nurse! You can say, "This is just absurd!" These people who blow our cover like this, we call them "gurus."

The fifth and last quality regarding why we meditate is what I call "no big deal." It's what I am getting at when I say we become "flexible" to the present moment. Yes, with meditation you may experience profound insight, or the magnificent feeling of grace or blessing, or the feeling of transformation and new-found courage, but then: no big deal. You're on your deathbed, and you have this nurse who's driving you nuts, and it's funny: no big deal.

This was one of the biggest teachings from my teacher Chögyam Trungpa Rinpoche: no big deal. I remember one time going to him with what I thought was a very powerful experience from my practice. I was all excited, and as I was telling him about this experience, he had a *look*. It was a kind of indescribable look, a very open look. You couldn't call it compassionate or judgmental or anything. And as I was telling him about this, he touched my hand and said, "No . . . big . . . deal." He wasn't saying "bad," and he wasn't saying "good." He was saying that these things happen and they can transform your life, but at the same time don't make too big a deal of them, because that leads to arrogance and pride, or a sense of specialness. On the other hand, making too big a deal about your difficulties takes you in the other direction; it takes you into poverty, self-denigration, and a low opinion of yourself. So meditation helps us cultivate this feeling of no big deal, not as a cynical statement, but as a statement of humor and flexibility. You've seen it all, and seeing it all allows you to love it all.

Part One

THE TECHNIQUE OF MEDITATION

*When you sit upright but relaxed in the posture of meditation,
your heart is naked. Your entire being is exposed—to yourself,
first of all, but to others as well. So, through the practice
of sitting still and following your breath as it goes out
and dissolves, you are connecting with your heart.*

—CHÖGYAM TRUNGPA RINPOCHE

1

PREPARING FOR
PRACTICE AND MAKING
THE COMMITMENT

There are very few things you need in order to begin a meditation practice. In fact, all you need is you. Sometimes people think they need to sign up for a retreat or buy tons of meditation-room supplies. But you can begin anywhere, in any room, at any time of day. You simply begin. You start where you are. You might feel that you are the single most stressed-out person on Planet Earth; you might be hopelessly in love; you might have six children and a full-time job; you might be going through a depression or a dark night of the soul. Wherever you are, you can begin there. You don't need to change a thing in order to start a meditation practice.

When you decide to become a regular practitioner of meditation, it's wise to settle on a schedule ahead of time. The fruits of meditation are manifold, and you really begin to see them and feel them when you practice regularly. So first and foremost, choose a schedule that is realistic for you—and then keep it. For example, decide what time of day you are going to practice. Perhaps it works best for you to practice in the early morning, before you have breakfast and get ready for work. Perhaps it works best for you to practice after your kids are in bed at night. Decide when you are going to get into a regular habit of meditation—and commit.

Next, consider how long you will practice. How long will you sit for? You can sit for twenty minutes or two hours; this is up to you. But set yourself up for success. When you commit to a meditation practice, you don't want to put yourself in a position where you will easily feel defeated. For beginning meditators, I suggest starting with twenty minutes. Then after a month or several months of practice, you can lengthen your time by another twenty minutes. If you are a seasoned meditator or if you are returning to a meditation practice, you might commit to an hour a day.

Perhaps you have an hour for your meditation practice, but sitting for more than twenty minutes feels daunting to you. If this is the case, I suggest sitting for twenty minutes, then perhaps taking ten minutes to slowly walk in a quiet, contemplative fashion, or to practice slow yoga, or to simply stretch. Reenergize yourself and give yourself a break through movement. Shifting your focus to something body oriented might help you to sit again for another twenty minutes.

Ideally, the environment for meditation is as simple as possible. It is simple in the sense that it does not require a great deal of setup. As you will discover, meditation is about letting the world in and awakening to your life, which means you can even meditate on a bus! But for the purposes of creating a regular practice, find a space in your home that feels sacred or relaxing for you. You might decide to create a little altar, a display of reminders that you feel supports your practice. You might want to place a picture of a teacher whom you connect with on your altar, or a candle, or perhaps some incense.

Next, consider your meditation "seat." As you will learn in the chapter on posture, you want to sit in a way that allows you to feel lifted—and this can be done on a cushion or a chair. Some choose to use what is called a *gomden,* which is a hard, square seat that lifts you up so your knees are below your sacrum. You can also use a *zafu,* a circular cushion, which is a bit softer and lower. Find the cushion or seat that works for you. If you have a bad back or a lot of knee pain, you can sit in a chair.

Last, find a timer. This can be a wristwatch, an alarm clock, or anything you can set that will alert you when the time you decided on is up. In meditation halls and on retreats, a gong (or bell) is often used, which is an extraordinarily gorgeous and peaceful sound.

You might practice alone, or you might decide to begin a meditation practice with a partner or a group. If you are a beginning meditator, I often recommend practicing with one or more people, because this will provide you with a great deal of support. You'll find that if you go at it alone, it is much more difficult to keep the schedule. The time-honored way of doing meditation is very often to practice alone, and in that case the commitment and devotion to a schedule can be more difficult, but I've found it gets easier as time passes.

Once a college student who came to me asking for instruction on how to meditate said that he experienced a lot of anxiety. He also had ADD (attention deficit disorder). This young student was longing for relief from all the stress in his life. He was also concerned about how he was going to integrate meditation into his busy life, with all his studies and obligations. I suggested that he meditate just ten minutes a day first thing in the morning, before even getting out of bed. I told him he could sit up in bed or on the side of the bed, cross-legged or legs extended, however he felt comfortable.

He came back after one week and said that this had really been helpful. He said that one morning he woke up really early, around 2:30 a.m., and he was having a panic attack because he had so much to do. His instinct was to jump out of bed and get to it, work on his huge list of to-dos. And then he remembered his commitment to start his day with ten minutes of meditation. So at 2:30 in the morning, he sat up and entered his meditation practice. In that experience, he said everything slowed down, and he was able to look at his wild, intense mind and his energized body. By being present with himself for those ten minutes, he had clarity about how to mindfully work through his list and see what needed to be done and in what order. The meditation allowed him to settle down and organize what he needed to do with clarity. It occurred to him that many of the things he felt he had to do actually didn't need to be done that particular day—and this settledness allowed him to return to sleep and feel much more refreshed when he awoke again at a more reasonable hour.

So perhaps you only have ten minutes that you can commit to meditation. Just ten minutes can help you come to your senses or slow down enough that your natural intelligence, or what I call basic goodness—the part of you that knows what the right action at any given time might be—can click in.

In this book, we are practicing what is called *shamatha*. Shamatha is a Sanskrit term that means "calm abiding." It is the practice of stabilizing the mind, training the mind to be present, settling the mind in the here and now, awakening to the world just as it is. In the following chapters, you will learn everything you need to know in order to start your shamatha practice: how to settle into your meditation space and enter your practice, how to sit and position your body, how to work with your breath, and how to work with the wild mind. As you know, a calm mind doesn't happen very often! But when you have an object of meditation that you keep coming back to—and in this book I teach that you begin with the breath— you are taming and soothing your mind and changing the habitual patterns where you are totally run by your thoughts and emotions. Placing the mind on an object is the backbone of shamatha practice.

2

STABILIZING THE MIND

Whenever you sit down to meditate, the first thing you do is settle. Settling means that you come into the room where you intend to practice meditation and you allow yourself to be completely as you are. You check in with yourself. You have a sense of being here and knowing what you brought in with you. Perhaps on one particular day you have felt very quiet since breakfast; perhaps you were looking out at the ocean or at the trees outside your window, and you actually come to your meditation quite settled and still. Other times you may feel rushed: you gobbled your breakfast and ran up and down the stairs, and you arrive at your meditation feeling all wound up. Maybe something happened last night or after breakfast that has you worried and upset, and so you're completely churned up. Maybe you're really tired, so you feel like you're hardly there. You might even feel dull or a sense of sinking.

One thing we can say for sure is that whenever you make time to sit down and practice meditation, you bring something along—you bring your thoughts and joys from the day with you, your disappointments and your concerns. The idea isn't to just plunk down and start your timer and block out everything that you've brought with you. So first, have some sense of where you're at. Ask yourself the questions: What am I feeling physically? What is my mood? What is the quality of my mind? So step one in getting settled is to check in with yourself.

The point is that there's not a good way to come into meditation or a bad way to come into meditation. It might feel preferable to show up feeling calm and spacious, but really meditation is about being awake and present to whatever is going on. You can't critique your meditation in terms of good and bad. The only thing you can measure your meditation against is the question: "Was I present or not?" And even then, to say to yourself that you weren't present is a result of the fact that you've been meditating and you recognized that fact. There's some sense of awareness about what is actually happening.

exercise

TOUCHING IN WITH THE PRESENT MOMENT

At the beginning of a meditation session, it can
be helpful to check in with your mind before
you begin. See where you're at right now. To find
yourself in the present moment, it can help if
you run through a series of questions to help you
contact your mind, to help you to become aware of
what's happening in this very moment.

So the first question is: What are you feeling?

Can you contact what you're feeling? It could be your
mood or your physical body, a quality of drowsiness
or peacefulness, agitation or physical pain—anything.
Can you contact that nonverbally and just
get a sense of what you're feeling?

To refine this question a little bit: Are there any emotions?
Can you be present to them? Can you contact them?

We're not talking about having to name anything
or remembering the history of the emotion, or
anything like that. Just be present to what you're
feeling right now.

Are you experiencing any physical sensations right now?
Pain, tightness, relaxation?

What about your thoughts? What's the quality of your
thoughts right now? Is your mind very busy? Is it quite
drowsy? Is it surprisingly still? Are your thoughts
raging or peaceful or dull? Obsessive or calm?

If I were to ask you personally, right now,
"What is the quality of your mind at this moment?"
Whether it's still or wild or dull,
whatever it might be, what would you say?

Hopefully these questions will help you touch in and make deep contact with yourself. I suggest that you begin your meditation practice with these questions. With practice, you'll find that you don't need to run through a list of questions to bring yourself into the present moment on your cushion. It will become more automatic. Your intention is to simply locate your mind and stabilize the mind as you launch into your practice.

exercise

BODY SCAN

An additional way that I find effective to check in with myself—and call myself into the present moment before I begin a meditation session—is to do a body scan. You can start by standing up and allowing for a deep inhale and exhale. You can do a complete body scan really quickly, and the idea is to place your mind on each body part so you can get a sense of how that body part feels in the present moment. So, for example, you might call yourself to the soles of the feet because you're standing, and you notice what is going on there. Perhaps your soles are numb; perhaps they feel awake and tingling. There will be parts of the body, as you go through it, that you probably won't be able to feel. If you get to pain, no problem—just allow yourself to notice and feel it. But still, place your open awareness on each part of the body. This is an exercise in mindfulness, an exercise in attention to the physical body.

So first, begin by standing for a minute. You can have your eyes open, or you can have your eyes closed. Just place your mind, your light, your gentle attention, on each part of the body. I like to allow myself about ten seconds of silence with each body part.

Start going through your body. The soles of your feet. The back of your ankles. Your calves. The back of your knees. The back of your thighs. Your buttocks. The lower back. Middle back. Upper back and shoulders. Your arms. Armpits. The back of the upper arms. Elbows. Back of the lower arms. The back of the hands. The palms of the hands. Back of the fingers. Tips of the fingers. The front of the hands. Front of the lower arms. Front of the upper arms. Your shoulders. Back of the neck. Back of the head. Back of the ears. Top of the head. Forehead. Eyes. Nose. Your cheeks. Your mouth. The lips. Tongue. Teeth. Your chin. Throat. Chest. Solar plexus. Stomach. Genitals. Front of the thighs. Knees. Shins. Top of the feet. The top of the toes.

Having done all that, see if you can feel now some sense of the whole body: standing, relaxed, maybe not so relaxed, but standing in the present moment.

3

THE SIX POINTS
OF POSTURE

At this point, you've stabilized the mind as best you can. You've called your attention to the present moment. You're almost ready to begin the formal practice of meditation. But before you begin, how should you sit?

Always in meditation, in no matter what tradition you're taught, there's a lot of emphasis on a nice, straight posture so that you're not slumping and so the energy can move freely through your body. Attention to a relaxed yet strong posture is also conducive to comfort. The way I've been taught to attend to posture during meditation is to keep my heart open—open heart and strong back. Actually it's a gesture of enormous bravery to sit up when you find yourself slumping, when you find yourself closing down. You can actually help your mind and heart to open by sitting with an open front. So the head and the torso, which is from below your neck to your waist, is like a straight line that just drops from the top of the head down through your body. Whenever you find yourself slumping, just lift up again. Open your heart.

Good posture for sitting meditation—a posture that allows us to be relaxed and settled in our bodies—involves attention to six points: seat, hands, torso, eyes, face, and legs.

SEAT

To begin, you want to find a nice, stable base. Sometimes I call it a flat bottom, but it's basically just a stable base. People sit on different things: some people sit on the flat ground, some people sit on gomdens, some on zafus, some on chairs. We each need to find our own way to this sense of being well balanced. We each need to find a good base.

HANDS

The hands, generally speaking, are in the "resting the mind" mudra, which involves just resting them on your thighs, palms down. If the hands are too far back on the thighs, then it pulls your body out of alignment, which can add stress and pain to your sitting posture. Also, if the hands are too far forward it pulls your body out of alignment. You have to find your own place of comfort where you feel well aligned, so that the torso is upright and comfortable and you're not leaning forward or backward.

If you are feeling drowsy, an alternate posture for your hands could be the Zen mudra, where you place one palm over the other and you make an oval shape by joining your hands. The thumbs almost touch, but not quite. You don't let your hands sit in your lap, but instead you hold them up a little bit. This particular mudra is extremely helpful if you're spacey or tired because you need to have a little more awareness to hold the hands up and keep the thumbs from touching. The Zen mudra keeps you more alert.

Notice what works for you with the hands: you can use the Zen mudra to wake yourself up, or you may just prefer the "resting the mind" mudra.

TORSO

When we talk about the torso, we want to think of relaxation as much as possible. To be upright, but also to be relaxed. I was taught to visualize a straight line that starts at the top of my head and goes straight down into the cushion. If I had a sense that this straight line was tilting forward or bending over or becoming somehow crooked, then I would remind myself to lift up again.

I was often given the instruction to have a sense of an imaginary string at the top of my head that was lifting me up. This image can be quite helpful because it often brings a feeling of lightness and relaxation to the body. But you have to be careful that your shoulders don't lift up as well. Be aware of your shoulders, and sometimes you can actually purposefully lift them and then drop them down—that's an old yoga trick—and that can help relax the shoulders, an area of the body where we have a strong tendency to tighten up.

The positioning of the torso is an expression of being awake and attentive. The front of your body should remain open with a strong back, and the whole body should be as relaxed as possible. So right now when you're settling in, if you feel that your shoulders are lifted up and tense, try to drop them. Relax. If your body is bent over so that your heart area and your stomach are collapsed, lift yourself up so there's a sense of uprightness and energy, which is held in balance with relaxation.

And again: keep the heart open. When we get tired, we tend to hunch over and close down in the front of our body and in our heart, whether we're doing meditation, sitting at our desk, or having a meal. By opening the front of the body, we often feel a sense of lifting up. It allows for the winds of moods and feelings to flow through the body much more easily. And if your posture is upright and the winds of experience move through your body with ease, then your mind can settle much more easily.

EYES

Often I notice meditators practicing with the eyes closed, but I suggest that you meditate with the eyes open, even if you're used to meditating with eyes closed. Open the eyes, because it furthers this idea of wakefulness. We are not meditating in hopes of going further into sleep, so to speak. We're not internalizing. This isn't a transcendental type of meditation where you're trying to go into special states of consciousness. Rather, we meditate to become completely open to life—and to all the qualities of life or anything that might come along. We are training in a kind of ultimate equilibrium or equanimity, which is not based on the outer circumstances being still, but on the mind being able to be flexible and open. We are cultivating the ability to stay present with whatever is coming up on the outside or on the inside—whether it's churned-up emotions or difficult outer circumstances.

There are many meditation traditions that encourage closed eyes—but the closed-eyes approach does not encourage the sense of presence in the moment that we are seeking. The tradition of closing the eyes comes more from the Southern tradition of Buddhism—the Theravadan tradition—and the intention with this kind of practice is a more internalized sense of meditation. In some of the traditions that instruct meditation with closed eyes—such as Hindu traditions—what is being cultivated is a kind of bliss state, or a rising-above kind of state. Tibetan Buddhism, in particular, is about being awake to whatever is arising.

Keeping your eyes open leads you toward the recognition that every moment and every place is the sacred world, and each one offers an opportunity to awaken to your life. With eyes open, you remain gently alert to whatever is going on rather than withdrawing, which is what happens when we close our eyes. Keeping the eyes open is very significant in terms of generating a sense of all-inclusiveness, which is where we learn to feel settled in our life no matter what storms or joys pass through.

So keeping the eyes open actually demonstrates this intention to stay with the present. It is a gesture of openness. We include whatever might occur during our meditation session; we're not looking around the room or allowing ourselves to become distracted. Often during group practice, people will be sitting next to you and in front of you, and there might be movement. There are visual things of all kinds happening in the room, and our meditation is designed to lead us toward being able to accommodate whatever might occur, rather than creating a situation that's totally free of any obstacles. We're opening toward working with the obstacles as path, rather than trying to be free of any obstacles.

I suggest that you place your gaze downward about four to six feet in front of you. If your mind is very wild and you want to find more stability, experiment with setting your gaze a bit closer. However, the head doesn't bend over; the head is always positioned as if you were looking straight ahead. But the eye gaze can be quite close in, as if you were looking right down your nose.

You can experiment with different eye gazes. The one I just described is close in. You can also set your gaze farther out, which is a more raised gaze. When you use a more raised eye gaze, you will see colors, you will see movement, and you will be aware of the light in the room—and that's intentional. You can experiment with maintaining a short, soft focus with whatever is around you.

FACE

Allow your mouth to be slightly open—just slightly ajar so that the air can move equally between the nose and the mouth. It's not wide open. Another person wouldn't really even notice your open mouth. This is actually quite helpful, because it relaxes your jaw.

Keeping your mouth slightly open also relaxes the face and the neck—and in that way also relaxes the shoulders. You will often notice if and when you get tense because your jaw might clench. If this happens, just notice that and let your lips part ever so slightly—so it is not even visible. Sometimes I give this instruction and I look out and I see all these gaping mouths—a room full of fish! That is not the idea.

In meditation, we put a lot of emphasis on trying to minimize a sense of struggle. We go through a lot with meditation—physical discomfort and mental discomfort—because everything comes up, and so we put a lot of emphasis on not struggling. So if you're hurting, you can make slight adjustments to try to get comfortable in your body. Notice if your face or your mouth is holding tension in any of the tiny muscles. Notice, and then let the tension go.

LEGS

The legs should be crossed comfortably in front of you. Sometimes people need to raise their seat because their legs don't go down. Sometimes people can sit completely flat. But however you sit, you don't want your knees to be higher than your waist because that will really cause you a lot of pain.

If the cross-legged position is nothing but painful for you—or if it exacerbates any injuries—I suggest you use a chair. Even if you sit in a chair, you can still work with the other five points of posture. Sit in the chair with your spine erect, heart open, palms on your legs, and your face, mouth, and gaze relaxed.

At any time during a meditation session, you can always, as Trungpa Rinpoche used to say, "Flash back to your sense of being." If you find yourself getting spacey or if you feel tension growing in your body, you can come back to awareness of your body and these six points of posture. First, recall the seat—the well-stabilized seat. You are not tilting forward or backward. You've found a nice base for an upright posture. Next, call attention to your hands, relaxed, on your thighs. Then your torso, which should be a straight back with an open heart, allowing energy to move freely through your body. Then the face: Is your mouth slightly open, and are the muscles in your face relaxed? And last, your legs, crossed in front of you: Can you let go of the tension in your legs?

If during your meditation you find that you are somehow struggling physically, don't move right away. Stay with it a little bit longer, and then slowly move yourself into a more relaxed posture as you continue your meditation. Bring ease to your posture. It's so important not to get into a major struggle but to simply try to be as relaxed and comfortable as you can. In each of these six points, you want to embody a sense of relaxation, openness, and dignity; you want to embody an expression of being awake and confident.

4

BREATH

The Practice of Letting Go

Breath practice trains us in letting go. It brings gentleness to our practice, and through the breath we are able to relax and unwind. Focus on your breathing, just for a few moments, and see if that helps you to soften. Just allow yourself to feel the sensation of the breath coming in, and going out.

The instructions for sitting practice are very simple: you've come into your meditation room, you've set the timer, you've stabilized your mind as best you can, you've taken your posture, and you are gently going to place your mind on your breath. In meditation, I teach students to begin with the breath as the object to come back to. The breath is used as a basic object of meditation for many reasons, but one excellent reason is because it's impermanent. It's always changing; it's always flowing; it's not a stable thing. By focusing on the breath, you're feeling something rather than concentrating on something. And you're also developing your mind, training

37

your mind, to be able to stay present to the impermanence of things—impermanence of thoughts, impermanence of emotions, impermanence of sights and sounds, all the things that don't stay stable.

So when you sit, place your attention on your breath. Whenever your attention wanders, bring it back to the breath. With as much precision and clarity as possible, come back to its flow in and out. This is not watching the breath like a hawk; this is not concentrating on the breath. This is *feeling* the breath, or any word that you can use to describe being one with the breath. Let yourself be breathed in and breathed out.

Once when I was giving meditation instruction to a young woman and I was describing this idea of finding oneness with the breath, she used the word "allow"—allowing the breath to go in and out. I thought that word really captured the feeling of what we're doing with the breath in meditation, because "allowing" has such a gentle and nonclinging feel.

To take this even further, you can experiment with focusing your attention on the out-breath and the space that exists at the end of the out-breath before you breathe in again. Trungpa Rinpoche used to describe this focus as "mixing the breath with space." The breath comes in, you might then feel a slight pause or waiting or gap, and then you place your attention on the outwardness. When the breath goes out, you stay with that out-breath for as long as you can. Allow the breath to flow out in a very light, relaxed way.

Trungpa Rinpoche taught his students to practice with focus on the out-breath in order to emphasize opening to the world and letting go of our fixations. There can be a sense that while the breath goes out, you become part of the vast, open space around you. It's a very spacious and allowing feeling.

As you work with the breath as your object of meditation, you will begin to feel your body and mind becoming synchronized. You are no longer divided. You can call meditation practice the "practice of open awareness" or the "practice of natural wakefulness."

As your practice grows, you can lighten your attention on the breath, allowing yourself to calmly abide in the open space of the present moment. What does it mean to sit and "be present"? It means to be like space itself, allowing everything that arises—breath, thoughts, emotions, sensations, everything.

5

ATTITUDE

Keep Coming Back

Now that we have the basics down—getting settled, posture, and breath—you have all the tools you need in order to meditate. Now let's touch on the basic attitude. We will look into the finer details of attitude and working with thoughts and emotions in Part Two, but to begin with, what attitude should we take when we meditate?

During meditation, we maintain a simple attitude, and that's the attitude of "keep coming back." The basic frame of mind we want to take is that we should always come back and be present. The basic instruction is to bring out the stabilized quality of mind—the ability of mind to stay in one place, to stay present. This is the basis of all the transformation that the meditation path produces in us. It begins when our mind can stay. Our mind can take us to the most outrageous places, and meditation teaches us to recognize exactly what is happening when our mind takes us away from the present moment. It can be very subtle, and it can be very dramatic and charged. We notice it, and we come back to the breath, back to our meditation. The natural quality of mind is clear, awake, alert, and knowing. Free from fixation.

By training in being present, we come to know the nature of our mind. So the more you train in being present—being right here—the more you begin to feel like your mind is sharpening up. The mind that can come back to the present is clearer and more refreshed, and it can better weather all the ambiguities, pains, and paradoxes of life.

I began this book with a discussion on suffering as one of the reasons that people come to practice. We meditate in order to remove the root of suffering. Getting at the root of suffering begins with returning to the present moment, with coming back to the breath. This is where expansion can occur. Expansion won't happen if you try to push through or escape your meditation. It won't happen by resisting what is present for you in the moment. The present moment, you will find, is limitless. It seems paradoxical that expansion and settledness can happen as we learn to return to the present moment, especially when what comes up in the present moment is anger or sadness or fear. But it is precisely through this act of coming back to the present that we can open to love and joy and the dynamism of life. In other words, meditation brings us the blessing of equanimity, or emotional balance. Meditation and the dharma directly address the tension and stress that are associated with much of our life. We might call this one of the "fringe benefits" of meditation.

The root of suffering escalates into full-blown suffering when we go on and on with our habitual emotional reactivity, when we let ourselves get carried off by our thoughts and sto-ries. There are many ways to talk about the root of suffering, but I often describe it as ignorance, because that's very easy to understand. With meditation, we are addressing the qual-ity of ignorance, or not knowing. The quality of not knowing refers to this phenomenon of not being aware, of not under-standing what it is that we're doing in our everyday life. This includes the smallest details of our life, such as not being aware that we're drinking a glass of water or spacing out when we're brushing our teeth. These everyday acts that we often do quite mindlessly can exhibit a lack of awareness, or ignorance. When we multitask and split up our mind into a million directions, we are actually creating our own suffering, because these habits strengthen strong emotional reactivity and discursive thought.

By accepting and living in the present moment, just as it is, we begin to experience more contentment, more spaciousness, and much less fear and anxiety and worry. Meditation works very directly with beginning to see what we're doing and begin-ning to realize that we have a choice in any moment to either return to the present or to escalate our suffering by letting our stories and thoughts take over. In any given moment, whether on the meditation cushion or in postmeditation, we begin to perceive more and more clearly—because of our meditation practice—how we are getting hooked, how we're attaching to a line of discursive thought, which is disastrous in terms of strengthening habitual patterns of suffering. We begin to see this more and more clearly, and we begin to realize that we can do something different.

A wonderful example of this comes from a student who told me a story about looking in the mirror and noticing that she had some gray hairs. She'd been in a contented mood, yet from that one simple observation she began a downward cycle of self-denigration and a familiar cycle of feeling very bad and low, very lonely and unloved. And this whole thing started from just seeing a grey hair! But because of her meditation, she saw what she was doing, caught it in its tracks, and she didn't go on the downward cycle. She noticed where her thoughts were taking her, and she came back to her breath. She took this attitude of coming back. Back to the present moment.

The more we see this kind of pattern and don't go on the downward cycle, the more our confidence grows in our capacity to awaken. As we expand our confidence in the workability of our situation, we begin to see that we are not victims of our habitual patterns. It can definitely feel like we are victims of our habitual patterns; they have a very sneaky way of getting the better of us. But the path of meditation addresses these patterns very directly, and it begins to unwind this whole sense of being imprisoned by our own mind.

The mind is the source of all suffering, and it is also the source of all happiness. Think about that. In fact, you can contemplate this for the rest of your life. When something comes up in your life that causes you dissatisfaction, or triggers habitual patterns and reactivity, or makes you angry, lonely, and jealous, ask yourself: Are these emotions happening because of outer circumstances? Are they completely dependent on outer circumstances?

The path of meditation says that we have to work with our mind, and that if we do work with our mind, the outer circumstances become workable. Things that used to irritate and bother us or that trigger our reactivity and habitual patterns begin to dissolve. So whenever you find yourself caught in an emotional attack, you have to ask yourself: "How much of this is really happening on the outside, and how much of this is my mind?"

I really challenge you to ask this kind of question every moment, every second of your day, and every day of your week, and every week of your month, and every month of your year. I really urge you to work on this. And you can do it in the manner that the Buddha suggested, which is that we look closely at where our fears and suffering originate. This is different from closing our minds to what is happening, the details of a scenario, and saying, "This is ridiculous—this is *clearly* Tim's fault." Or, "If those people in the office could just get it together then I wouldn't be having this problem." This is challenging because our experience of our minds can feel so true, so real. Meditation allows us to see the suffering our minds inflict on us.

The guideline is this: if you're hooked, then you need to work on your side of the situation, no matter how outrageous and unjust the outer circumstances might seem. If you're hooked, this is a clue that you have some work to do—and you, only you, can call yourself back. This is the basic attitude of meditation.

6

UNCONDITIONAL
FRIENDLINESS

Whenever we practice meditation, it is important to try to refrain from criticizing ourselves about how we practice and what comes up in our practice. This would only be training in being hard on ourselves! I want to emphasize the importance of maintaining an atmosphere of unconditional friendliness when you practice and as you take your practice out into the world. We can practice for a lot of years—I know many people who have practiced for countless years, decades even—and somewhere along into their umpteenth year, it dawns on them that they haven't been using that practice to develop lovingkindness for themselves. Rather, it's been somewhat aggressive meditation toward themselves, perhaps very goal-oriented. As someone said, "I meditated all those years because I wanted people to think I was a good Buddhist." Or, "I meditated all those years out of a feeling of *I should do this, it would be good for me.*" And so naturally we come to meditation with the same attitudes with which we come to everything. I've seen this with students time and time again, and it is very human.

Rather than letting this be something to feel bad about, you can discover who you are at your wisest and who you are at your most confused. You get to know yourself in all your aspects: at times completely sane and openhearted and at other times completely messed up and bewildered. We are all at times a basket-case. Meditation gives you the opportunity to get to know yourself in all those aspects. Judging ourselves for how our practice is going or what might be coming up for us during meditation is a kind of subtle aggression toward ourselves.

The steadfastness we develop in meditation is a willingness to stay. It may seem silly, but meditation actually isn't too unlike training a dog! We learn to stay. When you're thinking about what you're going to have for lunch, you "stay." When you're worried about what's going to happen on Monday, you "stay." It's a very lighthearted, compassionate instruction. It is like training the dog in the sense that you can train the dog with harshness and the dog will learn to stay, but if you train it by beating it and yelling at it, it will stay and it will be able to follow that command, but it will be extremely neurotic and scared. As long as you give a very clear command in the way that the dog was trained, it will be able to follow it. But add in any kind of unpredictability or uncertainty, and the poor animal just becomes confused and neurotic. Or you can train the dog with gentleness. You can train the dog with gentleness and kindness, and it produces a dog that can also stay and heel and roll over and sit up and all of these things—but the dog is flexible and playful and can roll with the punches, so to speak. Personally, I prefer to be the second kind of dog. This staying, this perseverance, this loyalty that comes with meditation—it's all very gentle, or compassionate in its motivation. This gentle approach to yourself in meditation is called *maitri*. This is translated as "lovingkindness," or just "love." In terms of meditation, we learn to be kind, loving, and compassionate toward ourselves. I teach about maitri a lot, and it is often misunderstood as some kind of self-indulgence, as if it is just about feeling good and being self-concerned. People will often think that that's what I mean by maitri. But it's somewhat subtle what maitri is and what it isn't. For example, you might say that taking a bubble bath or getting a workout at the gym is maitri. But on the other hand, maybe it isn't, because maybe it's some kind of avoidance; maybe you are working out to punish yourself. On the other hand, maybe going to the gym is just what you need to relax enough to go on with your life with some kind of lightheartedness. Or it might be one of your sixty-five daily tactics to avoid reality. You're the only one who knows.

So it's important to be clear about what maitri means and not to come away with a misunderstanding of maitri as some kind of indulgence, which actually weakens us and makes us less able to keep our heart and mind open to ourselves and the difficulties of our life. I often use this definition: maitri strengthens us. One of the qualities of maitri is steadfastness, and that's developed through meditation. So through boredom, through aches, through indigestion, through all kinds of disturbing memories, to edgy energy, to peaceful meditation, to sleepiness, it's steadfastness. You sit with yourself, you move closer to yourself, no matter what's going on. You don't try to get rid of anything—you can still be sad or frustrated or angry. You recognize your humanity and the wide gamut of emotions you might be feeling.

When we cultivate maitri toward ourselves, we are also generating equanimity. Equanimity means we are able to be with ourselves and our world without getting caught in "for" and "against," without judging things as "right" or "wrong," without getting caught up in opinions and beliefs and solidly held views about ourselves and our world. Unconditional friendliness is training in being able to settle down with ourselves, just as we are, without labeling our experience as "good" or "bad." We don't need to become too dramatic or despairing about what we see in ourselves.

If you could see clearly for one week, and then—boom!—all your bad habits were gone, meditation would be the best-selling thing on the planet. It would be better than any drug, any spa, any hammock on a gorgeous island. It would be *the optimum thing* if you could just see these habits, and just through one week or even one year of clear seeing and perseverance, then be entirely free of suffering. But we have been developing our habits for a very, very, very long time. However many years old you are, that's how old those habits are. And if you have a belief in reincarnation, you are looking at many more years with these habits!

This is your chance. This little, short human life that you have is your opportunity. Don't blow it. Think about how you want to use this time. Meditation is a patient process of knowing that gradually over time, these habits are dissolving. We don't actually get rid of anything. We are just steadfast with ourselves, developing clearer awareness and becoming honest about who we are and what we do. In basic sitting practice, we befriend ourselves and we cultivate maitri toward ourselves. As the days, months, and years of our meditation practice pass, we also find that we're feeling more and more lovingkindness toward others and the world as well. When I was a young student of meditation, I received a lot of encouragement from my teacher. He always referred to unconditional friendliness as "making friends with oneself." This felt tricky for me, because I always saw and felt things within myself that I wanted to avoid, things that were embarrassing or painful. I felt like I was making enemies with myself, because so much of this difficult material would surface during my meditation. My teacher said that making friends with myself meant seeing everything inside me and not running away or turning my back on it. Because that's what real friendship is. You don't turn your back on yourself and abandon yourself, just the way you wouldn't give up on a good friend when their darker sides began to show up. When I became friends with my body, my mind, and my transient emotions, and when I was able to comfortably settle into myself more and more (and remember, this takes time), then staying in the present moment, in all situations, became more possible for me to do. I was able in meditation to return to my breath and stop beating myself up.

I still have meditation sessions when I think or stress or deal with heavy emotion the whole time. It's true. However, after all these years, I'm definitely a lot more settled, you'll be glad to know. Unlike before, the thoughts and emotions don't throw me. If I sit down and my mind is going wild or I'm worried about something, I can still touch in to a settledness that I feel with my mind and my body and my life. It's not necessarily because things are going so great. Life, as you well know, is a continuous succession: it's great, it's lousy, it's agreeable, it's disagreeable; it's joyous and blissful, and other times it's sad. And being with that, being with this continual succession of agreeable and disagreeable with an open spirit, open heart, and open mind, that's why I sit to meditate.

7

YOU ARE YOUR OWN
MEDITATION INSTRUCTOR

In the Tibetan Buddhist tradition that I teach, we sometimes use what is called a *lojong* slogan, or a short pithy
sentence, for reflection or instruction. Lojong is a contemplative practice in which we consider a slogan and contemplate
its meaning for our life. These lojong slogans are like proverbs
that help us look more closely at our mind and habits.

There is one lojong slogan that says: "Of the two witnesses,
trust the principle one." In other words, there are a lot of people
who will give you good advice, and that can be extremely helpful, but basically you are the only one who knows what's going
on in your practice. I've presented you with the basic tech-
niques of meditation—and only you can really know how you
are doing with the suggestions and instructions. You are the
principle witness to your life, and you have to begin to trust
your own insight into your mind in order to determine what
your practice might need at any given moment. In a sense,
we become our own meditation instructors. The meditation

instructor within is always with you, showing you exactly where you are at.

Though I suggest also working with a mentor, a teacher, or a spiritual friend of some kind, in any given meditation session—or at any time during the day—they can't see completely inside your practice. They can't necessarily see whether you're spaced out or too tense, too harsh or wandering all over the place, too caught up in your emotions. You're the only one who knows what mood you're in. You're the only one who knows how much spaciousness you feel, how much peacefulness you feel, how much settledness you feel—and in that sense you are wise enough to be your own meditation guide in this practice of meditation.

A teacher, for example, cannot point out to you when you've touched the present moment deeply or if your back is hurting too much and you should readjust. It is something that only you can feel inside. My teacher, Chögyam Trungpa Rinpoche, used to say, "OK, now we're going to meditate," and the meditation gong would sound. "Everyone take good posture. Be aware of your breath going out, coming in, going out. Just awareness, open awareness of your breath." We'd do that for maybe twenty minutes, and the gong would sound again to end the meditation. Then he'd say, "The only real meditation you did in that whole period was when I hit the gong at the end."

This is often so true. Everybody gets into position, earnestly trying to be there with their breath, and they struggle, struggle, struggle. Because the sounds, instead of being an object of meditation, distract them; the thoughts, instead of being an object of meditation, distract them. For many people, there's the beginning of meditation when the timer or gong sounds, and this experience lasts for a little while—and then they're gone. They've left their meditation. And then at the end of the session, when the gong or timer sounds again, they finally allow this deep, long exhale. So these moments when the gong sounds at the beginning and the end of the session are often the most poignant moments of meditation—and only you can feel and know that. Moments like this show us that when we get too caught up in technique and trying, we lose the point of meditation completely. As your own guide, you can catch these insights, these graces, when they show up in your practice.

When we try too hard to meditate, we can easily lose touch with the reason why we decided to meditate in the first place. So as I mentioned in the previous chapter, be a very kind teacher to yourself. You don't need to beat yourself over the head about what comes up, or whether you are "doing it right," or whether you've made your technique "just so." The point is that you notice how these innumerable potential distractions move into your experience. Meditation is about leaving behind the idea that we are doing it perfectly.

So when you approach your meditation, you do want to consider the space, get settled into your body, check in with yourself. You do want to connect to the six points of posture and your breath. But I would also say that the key meditation instruction that you should give yourself, as your own teacher of meditation, is to simply relax into what is. We don't need to *do* anything. We rest in the space between our thoughts and emotions, between our aches and pains and worries. There is incredible wisdom to this open, present space. We are opening to the wild display of surprising richness, the organic and unique display of the present moment. We aren't trying, trying, trying. We aren't controlling or attempting and efforting our way through it.

The ability to drop into the present is sometimes referred to as child-mind, because children, little ones, look at things that openly, from that degree of relaxation, from that degree of nowness. Can you remember what it was like as a kid, sitting under a bush and how that smelled, or what it was like going to your grandmother's and how her house or garden smelled, how her perfume smelled? Think of a child going to a museum and not having a clue that what they are seeing is a Picasso or a Renoir. Not a clue at all. Children just look with this kind of open awareness. If they're really little, they hardly even know what they're looking at, but they're open to the colors and shapes.

Meditation calls us to return to, or tune in to, this natural ability to be present and see and hear. To be conscious, really. You could call meditation a practice of being fully conscious, as opposed to being unconscious, lost in thought and wandering away, which is a pretty typical state. In this practice, we remain loyal to ourselves, just as we would want a teacher to be loyal to us when they guide us. Meditation accepts us just as we are—in both our tantrums and our bad habits, in our love and commitments and happiness. It allows us to have a more flexible identity because we learn to accept ourselves and all of our human experience with more tenderness and openness. We learn to accept the present moment with an open heart. Every moment is incredibly unique and fresh, and when we drop into the moment, as meditation allows us to do, we learn how to truly taste this tender and mysterious life that we share together.

Part Two

WORKING WITH THOUGHTS

The towns and countryside that the traveler sees through
a train window do not slow down the train, nor does
the train affect them. Neither disturbs the other.
This is how you should see the thoughts that pass through
your mind when you meditate.

—DILGO KHYENTSE RINPOCHE

8

THE MONKEY MIND

The nature of mind is to think. It's as natural for the mind to think as it is for the body to breathe, or for the heart to pump blood through the veins. The motivation behind meditation is not to get rid of thoughts, but to train the mind to reclaim its natural capacity to stay present. Mind can be placed on an object, or on an experience, and it can stay there.

In Part One, I suggested you begin your meditation practice with placing your mind on your breath. Usually when we try to do that for even a few seconds, the monkey mind, or the wild-horse mind, goes off and takes us to the other side of the world or to something that happened a decade ago. The reason we don't just do meditation all the time is because we can't, and that's because our mind is all over the place. Our mind needs training. But we're not training our mind to be better; we're training to bring out the mind's natural wakefulness. The way we do that traditionally, from the time of the Buddha onward, is to meditate. We come back to our breath, come back to our body, come back to our object of meditation.

I had an experience the other day—it was brief, and I was aware of it—where I totally lost contact with what I was doing for about four seconds. The moment I was in just disappeared, and I went on the ride of my wandering mind. I was thinking about something. I thought, "My gosh, what an amazing ability we have to just escape, to not be here. We've got *that one* down! We've got it down because we've been training in it for years. It seems automatic."

And when I teach this to groups, there are always people—very intelligent people—who bring up some very good questions. They say, "You have to prove this to us because from our experience mind naturally is discursive, mind naturally wanders. Isn't that how we are supposed to operate and think in order to live and create?"

The journey to answer this question is one of the things that attracted me to Buddhism. The Buddha said, "Don't just take what I say as true because I say it. Really test it with your experience." I found that this was true. It takes quite a while to see that you actually can be awake and present and live your life in a creative and engaged way without letting your mind wander all the time.

When you meditate and you notice that your mind has wandered away from the breath, away from the present moment, all you have to do is call yourself back by labeling all thoughts as "thinking." You don't push the thoughts away, exactly. Rather, you note them, and you return to the breath. As you meditate, simply acknowledge your awareness of thinking by saying to yourself, "thinking." Then return to the breath. The instruction is that simple.

9

THE THREE LEVELS OF
DISCURSIVE THOUGHT

Many meditation texts talk about three levels of discursive thought. In the first level, we're totally gone. Our thoughts take us far away from the present moment for a stretch of time. This is also referred to as fantasy. When you come back from these wandering thoughts, it's like walking into the room after having left it for a while; you've been somewhere else. This is the most obvious kind of discursive thought; it can be a completely illusory—even delusionary—experience.

When you come back from drifting away from the breath and say "thinking," there's a strong tendency to be harsh because you've traveled so far away from your meditation. Notice your tone of voice when you say "thinking." If your tone is harsh, if the word "thinking" feels equivalent to "bad" or is accompanied by depression or a sense of discouragement, notice that. This is a place where you can bring relaxation and gentleness into the practice. Say "thinking" to yourself with a friendly attitude.

In postmeditation, it's the same. Start noticing this sense of aversion or critical voice to your thoughts and actions, and just lighten it up. Give yourself a break. You can change that voice and be more gentle and more kind, more compassionate, toward this whole process of your life. The labeling of thoughts as "thinking" is actually training in developing an unbiased attitude.

Criticalness is an obstacle to meditation, and harshness is an obstacle to awakening. This tendency to be hard on ourselves does not come from the buddha nature, the basic goodness within all of us; it comes from the ego and our conditioning. We all have the seeds of this basic goodness within us—we only have to nourish them. Nourishing the basic goodness within includes not judging ourselves for all the wild thinking that takes place in our mind. We can't control how many thoughts we're going to have. And we can't control what the next thought is going to be. As you practice, try to be faithful to the instruction with a gentle attitude. We train in attention, but it's friendly attention. We train in labeling, but it's friendly labeling.

Trungpa Rinpoche suggested that you adopt a young, innocent attitude to bring your mind back from thinking. He equated this to when you're trying to get an infant to eat some food, and the baby's attention keeps wandering. You have to be sweetly repetitive with the baby, reminding the baby to eat, to see the spoon, and then you pop the food into the baby's mouth. You just try to keep bringing the baby's attention back.

Fantasy and far-gone thought is one level of discursive thought. The second level is being gone, but not completely.

You are maybe two or three sentences into a thought or story line, but you're not gone for long before you wake up and come back. You're not completely in a fantasy. You're just drawn off by a sound, for example, and then the mind follows on the sound. Or perhaps you are drawn off by the feeling of hunger, and you start thinking about what to have for lunch. You realize this quickly, and you come back.

In the case of the less far-gone thoughts, the instruction is the same. You are sitting in meditation posture, placing your attention on the breath; the thought comes, and without making it a big deal, you just come back. You're allowing for the buddha-nature quality of your mind to come forward and manifest and be more present. If you let the thoughts take you farther away from the present moment, you are training in discursiveness and distractedness. It takes time and commitment to counteract this very well-ingrained pattern of not being here. The average life is characterized by a few moments of presence, maybe one in every hundred moments. Recognizing these small going-offs is really important, because they certainly add up!

As you spend more days and weeks with your commitment to practice, it might seem that your mind wanders even more. Many people, even seasoned meditators, say, "I'm thinking more than I ever did before!" They feel like their distractedness and thinking are getting worse, rather than better. The fact is that before you started meditating and trying to develop mindfulness, you weren't aware of how many thoughts you have. Now you are, and that's why there appears to be more of them.

Becoming aware of the monkey mind is actually a very good sign; it indicates an increase in your awareness and your ability to see what's going on.

The third category of discursive thought includes the thoughts that don't draw you off at all. You're sitting, and you put your mind on the object of the breath, and you're staying with it; then there's this little vague conversation or in-and-out of thoughts that's happening on the side, but it doesn't draw you off. It's like you are a witness to the on-the-side vague hint of thoughts, but you don't enter them completely. In this case, you don't have to label the thoughts as "thinking," and usually you won't experience any criticism of yourself around these thoughts. It is important, however, to recognize this level of thinking in meditation, and to distinguish it from the kind of thinking that takes you to more faraway destinations.

As your meditation practice develops, you are likely to experience this third kind of thinking more often. You remain present to your meditation, you experience thoughts arising, but they don't draw you off. They're happening in the background, and you're still with the object, which is your breath. Remember, you don't need to struggle. You don't need to struggle to not have thoughts because that's impossible. So in the case of these background thoughts, say to yourself, "Good! This is fine, absolutely fine. I actually don't have to label anything here, and I don't have to try to sharpen this up. This is fine."

With all three levels of discursive thought, there are three words—three concepts—that might be a support for you in your meditation in terms of allowing yourself to relax around your thoughts. The first word is "gentleness," which I have already discussed. Have gentleness around the fact that you can't avoid thoughts; you can't control the fact that you'll be distracted, and you can't control how long you'll be distracted for.

The second word is "patience." Patience brings relaxation into your meditation, into your practice, into your life. You can't underestimate how helpful it is to be patient with yourself. You might have weeks where your thoughts take you on a complete roller-coaster ride. You might have an hour of meditation in which you never connect to your breath and you obsess about something from your past. The path of meditation is not a linear process. One day there may only be these little blurps of thought that don't distract you at all, and you think, "I'm really getting the hang of this! I feel so alive, so present." Then the next thing you know, you sit down and *bam!*—you're completely gone in a fantasy until the gong rings, and you get so frustrated that you feel like throwing yourself off a bridge.

Trungpa Rinpoche used to say that this kind of experience is very good because it humbles us. He said, "Our minds are great teachers because we have just enough growing awareness and alertness, or increasing kindness, to encourage ourselves." And as he pointed out, we can even get very arrogant about that. In other words, our humanity, this discursiveness and this inability to completely overcome the wild and drowsy mind, keeps us in balance.

The third word I'd like you to hold when it comes to your thoughts is "humor." Gentleness, patience, and a sense of humor. Have a sense of humor about the fact that your mind is like a wild monkey. In his book *Wake Up to Your Life,* Ken McLeod has a great quote from the Theravada meditation master Henepola Gunaratana. He says, "Somewhere in this process, you will come face to face with the sudden and shocking realization that you are completely crazy. Your mind is a shrieking, gibbering madhouse on wheels barreling pell-mell down the hill, utterly out of control and hopeless. No problem. You are not crazier than you were yesterday. It has always been this way and you never noticed." Our thoughts are like the weather—they're just passing through. In our practice, there's no need to cling to them, no need to see them as totally solid. They are thoughts, after all; they're not the present moment. Let them pass through the big sky of your mind.

10

THOUGHTS AS THE
OBJECT OF MEDITATION

In Part One, I offered basic meditation instruction, and I suggested that you make your breath the object of meditation. You place your attention on your breath, specifically the out-breath, and when your mind wanders you return to the breath.

As you start to get into a routine with your meditation practice, you can begin to play with using other objects for your meditation. For instance, you can actually use thoughts themselves as the support for wakefulness. It sounds counterintuitive, but thoughts can become a support for stabilizing your mind. And we have so many thoughts to work with!

Tsoknyi Rinpoche said that a good analogy for using thoughts as the object of your meditation is like being the doorman in an expensive, elegant hotel. The doorman opens the door and lets the guests in. The guests come in and then go out the other side, but the doorman doesn't follow them to the bathroom. Similarly, our thoughts come in and the thoughts go out, and we, the doorman, just open the door, notice them, close the door, open the door, notice, close the door. Thoughts come and thoughts go; they come and they go.

exercise

USING THOUGHTS AS AN OBJECT OF MEDITATION

Set a timer for a short fifteen-minute meditation period. To begin, run through all the points you learned in Part One of this book: allow yourself to get settled, find your posture, connect to your breath. For a brief minute, relax your body, relax your mind, and return to your breath.

Next, look at your mind. Notice your thoughts, and determine whether there are a few thoughts or many thoughts. Are they continuous flow-thoughts, or are there a few thoughts with a little space and then some more thoughts? Do you have a few sentences, a few paragraphs, then there's this sort of space, and after that the thoughts start again? Or is there a lot of space, then a few words, and then a lot of space? Do your thoughts create one continuous dialogue? Are you feeling tired and experiencing a lot of nonsense thoughts? Just notice. These are your thoughts, just as they are right now.

The intention is to place your mind on the thoughts
themselves, and the method for doing
this is just to observe.

When you are done observing your thoughts and how
they are working, just relax.

Mingyur Rinpoche points out that when you're just with the
mind and thoughts as an object, and then you go completely
unconscious and get swept away by them, you often have this
little "oops" moment when you call yourself back. He pointed
out that this "oops" moment is actually a moment of pure
meditation, a moment where you are totally centered in the
present moment. At this place, the mind just naturally comes
back. It's unforced. You could meditate for years and years and
you never make it happen. And yet it happens here in this
fresh, unmeditated moment of catching yourself to come back.
Thoughts will arise, and when they do, let those thoughts pass
through. It's a very radical notion that thoughts could be a
friend or an ally rather than an obstacle or something you
have to struggle with. When thoughts call our attention to
the discursiveness of our minds and call us back to the present
moment, I'd say they are worth the price of admission.

11

REGARD ALL DHARMAS AS DREAMS

Another lojong slogan that I like to work with when teaching meditation is: "Regard all dharmas as dreams." This is basically saying, "Regard all thoughts as being the same as a dream." This is considered a meditation instruction; it points out that as we sit in meditation, we could begin to realize that we create everything, all our thoughts, with our mind.

They are not solid. They are not something tangible that we can grasp onto. They are concepts, interpretations, made from our conditioning. In other words, whether we are thinking about a beach in Barbados or a lover or our spouse or what to eat for lunch, it might feel very real. But Barbados isn't in front of you, and lunch isn't happening until later.

So again, when we realize that this process is going on, we acknowledge it by just calling it "thinking." When we say "thinking," it's as if we're acknowledging that all our thoughts are like an illusion, or like a dream. The illusions that we create with our mind while we're sitting in meditation—illusions that we call "thought"—can create fear, joy, sadness, wonder, anger: the whole gamut of emotions. Thoughts can cause us to cry, they can cause us to smile. Many thoughts have a lot of emotional content. In our everyday lives, we are run around by these thoughts that we make so solid with our mind and our thinking. So when we say, "Regard it all as a dream," we lead ourselves toward something that many people have discovered throughout the ages about the nature of reality: it's not as solid as we think.

Coming to terms with the intangibility of our thoughts, with their lack of reality, can liberate us from enormous suffering and anguish. A thought or a fear can develop into a full-blown story line that can cause us incredible pain and upset. This tendency has the potential to destroy the quality of our life and our ability to connect with others. Our thoughts often escalate, and meditation helps us learn to de-escalate suffering. We make a huge deal out of our thoughts, but just like dreams, they have no real substance. They are like bubbles, or like clouds.

So when you realize you've been thinking, you can just touch the thought and let it dissolve back into the vast blue sky. You're not shooting down the thoughts like clay pigeons, and you're not cutting through the thoughts with a sword or smashing the thoughts over the head with a hammer. There's really nothing there to fight—you just let thoughts dissolve back into the vast blue sky, like touching a bubble with a feather.

Have you ever had the experience of waking up in a dream? It's called lucid dreaming, which means becoming lucid while in the dream state. It's quite a powerful experience if you wake up in a dream and actually realize that you're only having a dream. I've had some experience with lucid dreaming, and it's very interesting because once you begin to pay attention to these kinds of dreams, you realize that the way things appear often make it feel as though the dream is entirely real. If you throw something in a lucid dream, it drops and makes a noise and possibly breaks. You walk down streets and there's a whole landscape, and it's just like being awake. If you have continued experience with lucid dreaming, you begin to question if there is any difference at all between the waking state and the dreaming state.

Our thoughts are no different—they are just like dreams. And we can choose to wake up from them, to reenter the present moment where things are alive and vivid. We can give ourselves an enormous break by learning to let our mind relax, and not grasp and concretize things. We don't need to hold on so tightly with our mind, or make such a big deal out of our thoughts, or allow our thoughts to take us down some deep, labyrinthine rabbit hole.

When you say "everything is a dream," another way to say that is, "there is just so much room." We have an enormous amount of room to move around in. Our minds are really vast. We're not constricted by anything. But the opposite is our habitual experience. Our experience is usually quite claustrophobic, and we carry with us a very strong sense of burden, of things being solid. If we can loosen the grip of our thoughts, regarding them as dreams, we've just made the world and our ability to experience this world evermore larger.

Part Three

Working
with Emotions

So the intelligent way of working with emotions is to try
to relate with their basic substance. The basic "isness" quality
of the emotions, the fundamental nature of the emotions,
is just energy. And if one is able to relate with the energy,
then the energies have no conflict with you.
They become a natural process.

—CHÖGYAM TRUNGPA RINPOCHE,

The Myth of Freedom and the Way of Meditation

12

BECOMING INTIMATE
WITH OUR EMOTIONS

Working with emotions in meditation practice is a big subject for me. Very often, our thoughts are pretty lightweight. Just light, discursive thoughts. We're thinking, "What's for lunch?" or, "Did I remember to run the dishwasher this morning?" Sometimes we're just having the strangest thoughts. Perhaps you are having a memory of your grandmother eating raw onions. Where does that come from?

Sometimes these thoughts take you away. Usually they do. But many times, they don't have a lot of emotion in them. These little things passing through your mind come and go like the wind. You can get completely caught up in this fantasy world, but on the other hand, it's somewhat lightweight. When you realize you're thinking, you say "thinking." You let the thoughts go, and there you are in the present moment. Maybe it lasts only half a second.

But if you sit longer, the more you sit, then—no question—painful memories will come up. Suddenly you are struggling against how you're feeling, and a lot of emotion is involved.

The instruction I've been giving for years is: when you're meditating, and even in your everyday life, notice when you're hooked. Notice when you're triggered or activated. That's the first step: you acknowledge that emotion has arisen.

Next, I advise students to drop the story line and lean in. Just pause, and for a second connect in with spaciousness, with openness. I call this the "pause practice." It's like taking a time-out for yourself. Then you lean in to the quality or the texture or the experience, completely touching in to the emotion, without the story. How does the sadness feel? How does the anger feel? Where is it in your body? You let the feeling of the emotion become the object of your meditation. And the reason that I've been so committed to teaching on this is emotion itself is a radical and very potent way of awakening.

Without a doubt, this is where everyone loses it. We have so much fear of our emotions, so much aversion to them. You get caught in the momentum of the emotion, and it sweeps you away as if you were in its control. But I've found that we can take another approach, which is to enter the emotions that arise in our practice. Emotions are actually very empowering; I call working with the emotions "accelerated transformation." When you experience difficult emotions in your sitting practice, and you let go of the words and the story behind the experience, then you're sitting with just the energy. And yes, it can feel painful to do this.

It's so funny, because sometimes when I give retreats, the TV cameras come in and take pictures of people meditating, and it looks like everyone's sitting there in complete serenity.

If you could see the speech balloons above people's heads, or feel what's going on with them, you might be knocked over in shock! The person next to you doesn't know that you're reliving a horror story from your childhood in graphic, heartbreaking detail, or that you're in a deep depression, or that you're having the world's most pornographic fantasy. What we look like and what's actually going on are often so completely different. We're just sitting there in a Buddha-like posture, and it might appear that we are experiencing nothing but openness and calm—and nothing could be further from the truth. But I think the Buddha had the same experience that we do. For him, as for us, meditation isn't always about sitting in a state of absolute calm. There is a scene in the movie *Little Buddha* where special effects are used to reflect the myriad emotions and temptations that are trying to seduce the Buddha. So much is coming at him—everything from gorgeous women to opportunities for power to things that are frightening, everything. The idea that the Buddha was completely chilled out and didn't experience emotion around any of these things simply isn't true. When the Buddha achieved enlightenment, he learned to be settled with all of those feelings coursing through him.

Like the Buddha, you can come to know your own energy, and you can feel quite settled with it. You become intimate with your own energy, and it no longer rules your life. Your conditioning doesn't go away, but it no longer controls you.

In many ways, it is critical that we do become intimate with our emotions. Sometimes it is even a matter of life and death. I want to tell you a story about my granddaughter. Her mother, my daughter-in-law, died of alcoholism at age forty-eight when my granddaughter was seventeen years old. The addiction had been going on for a long time, from the time my granddaughter was about two. Her mother had a recovery and was sober for ten years, but then she relapsed.

So my granddaughter was applying to college and she had to write an essay. One of the essays for the college was to write about a transformative experience, and the first line of her essay was, "My mother died on December 1, 2009." And this essay was so remarkable to me because in it she explained how her mother had died of alcoholism, and she said, "all my mother's friends from Alcoholics Anonymous were telling me, and I knew it to be true, that alcohol is a disease and once it has you in its grip it's pretty hard to shake it, and they said that's what happened with my mother." She said, "I knew that to be true, but I felt that her drinking was a symptom of something else. So while my mother was in the hospital in a coma, I wrote and wrote and wrote, trying to remember everything about my mother—my own memories, things she had said about herself, things her friends had said about her. I was trying to figure out who my mother was because I'm so much like her, and I wanted to figure out where she went wrong and what happened that ended in her dying so young."

In her essay, my granddaughter came to the conclusion that her mother had a fixed idea of herself as being a certain way. And one of my granddaughter's conclusions was that we're changing all the time; everything about us is always changing. My granddaughter said, "When you hold a fixed idea of yourself, you have to leave out all the parts that you find boring, embarrassing, difficult, or sad. You leave out the emotions you don't want to feel. And then when you do that, when you leave out all those parts, when those parts are not acceptable, then it eats away at you underneath. These unacknowledged parts are like a hum in the background that's eating away at you, and you have to find an escape to get away from that. And my mother's escape was alcohol."

In order for us to be fully present, to experience life fully, we need to acknowledge and accept all our emotions and all parts of ourselves—the embarrassing parts as well as our anger, our rage, our jealousy, our envy, our self-pity, and all these chaotic emotions that sweep us away. Looking for an exit from experiencing the full range of our humanity leads to all kinds of pain and suffering. Meditation gives us the opportunity to experience our emotions naked and fresh, free from the labels of "right" and "wrong," "should" and "shouldn't."

13

The Space within the Emotion

One of the lines that I really like in Gaylon Ferguson's book *Natural Wakefulness* is "Distraction is married to discontent." You could test this out in your own experience. There's nothing as real and direct and counterhabitual as being present, just as it is, with yourself just as you are, with your emotions just as they are. As difficult as that can be, the result of that training is nonstruggle: not rejecting your experience, fully engaged with yourself, with the world, there for other people. Another result of coming back to being with yourself, just as you are, is that emotions don't escalate.

Drop a stone in the water and what happens? The ripples go out. If the stone is big enough, it can rock a rowboat on the other side of the lake. It's the same, generally speaking, when an emotion arises and you acknowledge, "Oh, I'm getting worked up. Oh, my heartbeat is going faster. Oh, I'm feeling fear. Oh, I'm feeling resentment." Or just, "Oh, I'm activated, triggered." At that moment, when you acknowledge it, there's a space. Just by the very act of acknowledging or being present enough, conscious enough, you'll find that space—and in that space lies your ability to choose how you're going to react. You can either stay present with whatever it is you're feeling—with the intensity or heat or edginess or shakiness of the emotion—or you can spin off. You can be caught in the momentum and carried away, which usually means you start talking to yourself about what's going on. You churn it all up more and more, and it's like the ripples go out and out and out.

When you choose to reinforce the emotion, when you choose to exaggerate it, when you choose to let the emotion run you, to let the emotion carry you away, then a whole chain reaction of suffering starts. It just sets off an automatic chain reaction like those ripples. So in meditation, we train in letting the rock, the emotion, drop without the ripples. You stay with the emotion rather than turning to the automatic reaction, a reaction that has been habitual for you for years and years.

And believe me, two seconds of doing something so radical, so counterhabitual, of not setting off the chain reaction, completely opens your life to this working from the space of open awareness. And if you don't reject the emotions, they actually become your friends. They become your support. Your rage becomes your support for stabilizing, for returning the mind to its natural, open state. Emotions become your support for being fully awake and present, for being conscious rather than unconscious, for being present rather than distracted. That which has been an ogre in your life has the ability to just sweep you away—or it can become your actual friend, your support. It's a whole different way of living, a whole different way of looking at the same old stuff.

14

EMOTIONS AS THE
OBJECT OF MEDITATION

Emotions are the arising of the natural dynamic energy of life. Thoughts are also natural and spontaneously arising. Everything that happens is naturally occurring; you don't actually invent any of it. Something occurs and you can invite it in to become your friend, your support for awakening. Emotions don't have to be so evil and scary; they are just energy. We are the ones who ascribe the labels of "good" and "bad" to our emotions.

Even though we each have a unique experience with our emotions, emotions are a universal experience. When an emotion arises, everybody has the same choice. Everyone knows how to strengthen the old habits of anger, and everyone knows how to feel resentment and self-pity. We're very good at it. But at the same time, you're the only one having that emotion, and even though your friends and relatives might tell you what you're thinking and feeling, actually you're the only one who thinks those thoughts and feels those feelings.

So each emotion is unique, and it doesn't have to be called "good" or "bad" or anything at all. It's just as it is.

Take a few seconds to conjure up or get in touch with an unpleasant emotion. I would not recommend starting with something extremely traumatic! We all have totally incapacitating unpleasant memories or feelings. Get in touch with something along the lines of how miffed you were when someone took the last cookie. How upset you were when so-and-so interrupted you when you were talking. Begin with a mild irritation. By working with the "lightweight emotions," we build up strength, just like working out at the gym. You start where you are, and then you work out and your strength grows. So by using lightweight emotions (irritation or mild anxiety), believe it or not, it's building up your strength to work with really difficult emotions.

exercise

USING MEMORY AS A SUPPORT IN MEDITATION

Sit for a minute and find a painful memory that you
can use for this exercise. Maybe it is a memory
of being criticized. Sometimes people use a memory
or sometimes people use a visual image of
something that provokes them.

Next, find a pleasant emotion. Retrieve a memory or
a visual image that evokes a pleasant emotion, such as

being praised. Just for a moment, think of that. Have a memory or a visual image that feels positive.

With a painful emotion and a pleasurable emotion in mind, begin your meditation session. Place your mind on the breath, first allowing your breath to be the support. Let your breath be your friend for training in being present. If your mind wanders off, which it usually does, just come back to the breath. Do that for a short time, perhaps five minutes, and then rest in the open awareness.

Recall that anything can arise in space and be the object or support for your training. So now mentally fabricate or, using a memory or a visual, bring forward in your awareness the emotion that's unpleasant and place your attention on the emotion. See if you can contact the texture of the feeling. If someone asked you to describe the feeling of the emotion, how would you describe it? Fully put your attention on the emotion itself, just as it is.

Some people find it helpful to feel for the emotion's temperature or texture, or its location in the body. For some people this is very easy; for others it is quite difficult. Just do your best to be present with the unpleasant emotion. Do that for a short time, and then once again rest in open awareness.

If at any point your mind wanders off, gently bring it back without the labels of "right" and "wrong." Often our emotions take us into the story or the thoughts. When the thoughts arise, notice them, notice the thinking, then bring yourself to the feeling of the emotion. There, in the immediacy of the emotion, feeling into it, lies the possibility of moving into openness and acceptance. You'll find that this is quite liberating and eventually quite settling.

I encourage you to get curious about your emotions and to allow yourself to go into them so you can experience this opening. This is how the heart opens. This is how compassion arises—compassion for oneself and compassion for others.

Next, repeat the same exercise above, this time recalling a pleasant emotion.

No amount of talking on the part of a teacher is going to stop you from following the trail of your emotions as it moves from emotion to thought to escalating emotion. You need to go into your emotions; you need to sit in meditation with them yourself so you can begin to realize how they are obstructing you. Emotions are like the fluid, dynamic, living quality of water, but we freeze our emotions into ice by pushing them away or letting them escalate. We turn our emotions into frozen objects and invest them with truth, and as a result they have so much power over us. So we train again and again in coming back to the object of meditation as a way of interrupting that fixated quality. The grasping and fixation—that's really what we're interrupting.

I hope that as the years go on you become more and more motivated to do this whenever you notice that your monkey mind has been trailing off in dozens of directions. I hope that you feel strongly motivated to come back and uncover the true nature of mind. You're allowing yourself to connect with the natural, open state of your mind, and you're beginning to dissolve this ancient habitual pattern of fixating and grasping. Meditation helps us to interrupt this fixation with our emotions in a very nonaggressive, gentle, friendly way, because we invite relaxation and spaciousness into this process. We learn to recognize the fluidity of our emotions by going into them and letting them pass through like clouds in the sky.

15

GETTING OUR
HANDS DIRTY

I was reading a transcript of a talk by Ponlop Rinpoche, and he said, "In the process of uncovering buddha nature, in the process of uncovering our open, unfixated quality of our mind, we have to be willing to get our hands dirty." In other words, he was saying that we need to be willing to work with our disturbing emotions, the ones that feel entirely dark.

We all have emotional experiences that feel terrifying, and in order to experience our natural state, we have to be willing to experience these emotions—to actually experience our ego and our ego clinging. This may feel disturbing and negative, or even insane. Most of us, consciously or unconsciously, would like meditation to be a chill-out session where we don't have to relate to unpleasantness. Actually, a lot of people have the misunderstanding that this is what meditation is about. They believe meditation includes everything except that which feels bad. And if something does feel bad, you're supposed to label it "thinking" and shove it away or hit it on the head with a mallet. When you feel even the slightest hint of panic that you're about to feel or experience something unpleasant, you use the label "thinking" as a way to repress it, and you rush back to the object of meditation, hoping that you never have to go into this uncomfortable place.

But Ponlop Rinpoche added something really important to this statement. He said that without having a direct experience of our emotions, we can never touch the heart of buddha nature. We can never actually hear the message of awakening. The only way out, so to speak, is through. But what does this word "experiencing" mean? And how can we experience emotions? How can we experience this negative, disturbing, unsettling stuff that we generally avoid? How do we get our hands dirty with them?

Ponlop Rinpoche says, "It's only by really tasting your experience of emotions that you get a taste of enlightenment." Buddha nature and the natural state are not just made up of happy, sweet emotions; buddha nature includes everything. It's the calm, and the disturbed, and the roiled up, and the still; it's the bitter and the sweet, the comfortable and the uncomfortable. Buddha nature includes opening to all of these things, and it's found in the midst of all of them.

Because we perceive dualistically and have this black-or-white thinking where we label things either "good" or "bad," we shut down when strong energy arises. We associate this strong energy with different thoughts—memories of the past or fantasies about the future—and then this somewhat indescribable thing happens, which we call "feeling an emotion." Emotions, in essence, are just pure energy, but because of dualistic perception we identify the emotion as "me," and it gets very locked in. The energy gets frozen. Trungpa Rinpoche once said, "Emotions are composed of energy, which can be likened to water, and a dualistic thought process, which could be likened to pigment or paint. When energy and thought are mixed together, they become vivid and colorful emotions. Concept gives the energy a particular location, a sense of relationship, which makes the emotions vivid and strong. Fundamentally, the reason why emotions are discomforting, painful, frustrating is because our relationship to the emotions is not quite clear."

This is to say that energy itself is not a problem. We always associate our emotions with thoughts—we're scared of something or we're angry at somebody, or we're feeling lonely or ashamed or lustful in relationship with either ourselves or somebody else. Our emotions have a lot of mental conversation—and, in my experience, it is often hard to discern between what is the thought and what is the emotion. In any given sitting period; in any given half hour of our lives, there are a lot of things that come and go. But we don't need to try so hard to sort it all out. We don't have to attach so much meaning to what arises, and we also don't have to identify with our emotions so strongly. All we need to do is allow ourselves to experience the energy—and in time it will move through you. It will. But, we need to experience the emotion—not think about the emotion. It's the same thing that I've been talking about with the breath: experiencing the breath going in and out, trying to find a way to breathe in and out without thinking about the breath or conceptualizing the breath or watching the breath.

I often describe this as having a "felt sense" of our emotions. This term "felt sense" may not really be the right term for you. For instance, you could have an experience of dread; you likely carry a story line about being afraid of something that's about to happen. But if there is a way that you can interrupt the conversation through your meditation training, even for a few moments, then you can have an actual experience of dread—a nonverbal experience. You can allow yourself to become physically aware of dread. Feel it; feel the clenching and tightness. It can even go deeper than that: you might have a textural experience of dread as tingly or hot, a coldness or sharpness in your chest.

One of my first experiences of really feeling an emotion was very interesting. I was in a period of a lot of distress that I couldn't get away from. This happens in our life, frequently. The person who was triggering me wasn't going away. It was at the abbey, where I live. And we had to live with each other and in pretty close quarters, and what was being triggered were old memories and conditioning. This is often the case with strong emotions. There's a lot locked in us. It can be quite irrational. It's like we're dogs who hear certain sounds and freak out. We see a certain facial expression, or someone treats us in a certain way, or there's just the right tone of voice, or someone reminds us of something, and out of the blue there's this whole felt sense of dread or anger or deep sadness. Usually we're not even aware of it; we're simply reacting the way we always have.

In this particular instance, what was being triggered for me was a feeling of helplessness, because this woman disliked me intensely and wouldn't talk to me about it. The situation was bringing up feelings of powerlessness, of not being able to get things under control, of not being able to make everything all right. I couldn't get her to like me, and I couldn't even get her to talk about it. There was no way that my usual strategies were going to work, so I was just naked with this reoccurring dread. I met her in the halls constantly; she'd walk by coldly and, boy, it would bring up what felt like centuries of conditioning and perceived hurts.

I thought to myself, "This is my big chance. Maybe if I really go into this, I won't ever have this issue come up again in this lifetime or any other lifetime." So one night I went to the meditation hall. I sat all night long because I was in so much pain and I didn't know what else to do. I didn't think much at all, because I was in so much pain. Sometimes pain completely knocks thoughts out; you're sitting in the pain, and it's like you're speechless at all levels.

As I sat, I began to have this quality of experiencing what I was going through with this woman. I had a body memory of being a very little child, but it wasn't like I was remembering a traumatic experience or anything. I just realized—at a cellular level—that my entire ego structure, my entire personality, was designed never to go to this particular feeling. I began to experience a deep feeling of inadequacy, like I wasn't OK. I realized that what I was experiencing was a complete death to ego.

From that felt experience, I began to realize the power of getting sidetracked with words, of getting sidetracked with thoughts about our emotions. We get completely sidetracked with our strategies, which are always designed to move away from the felt experience. So whether it's a humdinger of an emotion, a kind of core pain to our ego structure such as mine was, or whether it's any strong emotion or even a more mild emotion, it's so easy for us to get stuck and wrapped up in the story and thoughts around the emotion. From there, the emotions escalate and enslave us.

You have to get dirty with your emotions. Meditation allows us to feel them, live them, and taste them completely. It gives us a lot of insight into why we do the things we do and why other people do the things they do. Out of this insight, compassion is born. This insight also begins to open the doorway to buddha nature and the complete, open spaciousness that's available when we're not blocking our feelings. Once I was able to allow myself to have a felt sense of my emotions, it was completely liberating.

As Ponlop Rinpoche said, "Until you begin to really relate with the unfavorable or the unpleasant things as part of your meditation—they're not the whole thing—but until you start working with them, you don't really have the quality of being on a path of awakening."

16

HOLD THE EXPERIENCE

Ajahn Amaro, a British dharma teacher, said, "That which is threatening to ego is liberating to the heart." What he was pointing at here is that we practice meditation because it's a means of unwinding and dissolving the habits that limit us so that we can open our heart. It is very counterintuitive—but when we feel an emotion that feels totally threatening and awful, it is time to hold the experience of it. As I mentioned, Trungpa Rinpoche said that the definition of emotion is energy mixed with thoughts. If you can let the thoughts go, or interrupt the conversation, then you have just the energy. But you have to watch this closely in your meditation practice: a strong emotion distracts your attention away from the breath; it doesn't distract your attention into the emotion. You would think a strong emotion would distract you from the breath into the emotion, but in fact what a strong emotion does is distract you away from the experience. That's what happens. A strong emotion arises, and then whatever we do next with our mind, or with our words, or with our actions, distracts us away from the energy.

In the past few chapters, I've been trying to point out the importance of experiencing emotions as part of our path to awakening, to living more wholehearted lives. This is something we do when we train in meditation, but it is also something we must do throughout the day, because emotions definitely tend to come up during what we call "postmeditation." Perhaps you are one of those people who sits down to meditate and everything feels smooth and nothing comes up. This happens for many of us, especially in the beginning of our practice. But as soon as you have a chore rotation at a retreat and you have to work with someone you don't like or you have a phone call you don't want to make, then up comes the raging emotion. Watch how your emotions can take you by the collar and control you in those postmeditation situations.

When a strong emotion arises, it distracts our attention. Let's just say we're practicing attention: we're practicing being present, just being relaxed and open, relaxing into the present moment. We're practicing, training, in being present. We're training in gentle, open attention to everything that's happening—mentally, visually, audibly. Complete openness to what is arising. But when strong emotion arises, the usual pattern is that it distracts us. In meditation, strong emotion distracts your attention away from the breath; you get completely caught in it, and you're off and running because it's all mixed up with your thoughts.

When this happens, we most likely move to some kind of strategy: we go to war and we move into aggression by creating a story line about "they" or "me" or "if only." We might look for ways to destroy, blame, get revenge. We begin plotting it all out. Or the strong emotion arises and we go into a strategy of seeking comfort. We run and hide from the emotion. We distract ourselves through TV or food or other addictive, pleasure-seeking behaviors. We might obsess about how we can get away from facing or feeling this particular thing. We might distract ourselves by turning to pleasant memories, or planning something in the future. Another way we might seek comfort is by building ourselves up by thinking about how good we are and how we're going to set so-and-so straight and how we're so right—and on and on and on. In all of these cases, these strategies are moving us away from the rawness, the realness, the immediacy of the actual experience.

Control is another way we respond to the arising of a strong emotion. We have our methods, or strategies, of trying to control the situation to get it to work out OK. Before we know it, we're feeling a lot of other emotions that are actually distractions from the original feeling that arose. For example, there's the initial discomfort that we're actually afraid of, and then maybe we get teary, or we get paranoid, or we get jealous or enraged or fearful. Our strategies to move away get really complicated. The strategies for escape can show up in so many ways—even illness can be one. I've had a lot of illness. Illness is not necessarily a strategy, but if you've been ill a lot, you might begin to use it as a strategy. A strong emotion comes up, and then you somehow collapse into your weakness. Your illness may be valid, but you can use it, too. Notice what you start saying to yourself when you feel an angry emotion. What happens next in terms of the kind of stories you tell yourself? Does your mind become very critical? And are you being gentle with yourself when the emotion comes up? When I work one on one with students, I often hear so much self-judgment when strong emotion arises for them in their practice. I hear things like "I never get it right" or "I can't do this" or "This is too hard." Either you blame yourself or you blame something else: "This technique is stupid" or "This is a waste of my time." We put ourselves through all kinds of negative thinking.

What I often tell students is this: simply abide with the experience without believing in the stories or opinions about it. Go into your body, and start breathing in and out while trying to simultaneously hold the experience. "Hold the experience" doesn't mean we're trying to pin it down. Rather, it is a brave act of becoming vulnerable and allowing our humanity. From this courageous act of holding the experience, a very natural warmth emerges, for ourselves and for all other beings.

I promise you that when you allow yourself to truly experience the rawness of your emotions, a whole new way of seeing the world, of experiencing love and compassion, will be revealed to you.

17

BREATHING WITH
THE EMOTION

When a strong feeling comes up, it will often be accompanied by a strong habitual pattern. These are the emotions where you automatically start to go into your justification or defense, or your story or search for pleasure, or whatever it is you do. This is where we really get stopped in our tracks on our path of awakening. This is also the very place where we could make enormous progress on the path if we're willing to allow our thoughts and emotions to become part of our path. When the emotion arises, go to the body and breathe in and out, and at the same time experience the emotion. If you just go to the breath without experiencing the emotion as well, this can be a way of repressing the emotion.

For example, anger comes up, and then you go to breathing as a way to chill out the anger. But you also want to really experience the underlying energy of anger until it no longer has this power over you. Chilling out helps a little bit—breathing in and out—but the anger will still be there to just pop out the next time the causes and conditions arise. It's there, just as strong, and you're just as afraid of it as ever—maybe even more afraid. Because every time you repress it, you're becoming more afraid of it; it's becoming more of an opponent. And it's bigger than you.

So experience the emotion. Breathing is a way of staying present; it anchors you. Because if you just go to the felt experience without the breath, my experience and the experience of other meditators has been that you can drown in it. This leads to overwhelm.

You need to breathe *with* the emotion; you don't breathe it away. If the emotion does dissipate, fine. That's what just happened—and it does happen. Let it be like that. But the point is to go to our experience rather than to go to our strategies or our conceptual ways of exiting. You're breathing the emotion in, and so you're being with it. You *are* it, actually. You could even imagine that you are breathing the emotion into the heart. Imagine you are breathing it into the heart—the large heart—if that helps you. Breathing the emotion in is the basis for empathy, for being able to stand in someone else's shoes. You're feeling anger or fear or jealousy or poverty, and then as you breathe in, there could be the recognition that billions and zillions of people feel this right this moment, and they have felt this in the past, and they will feel this in the future. You're touching into a universal experience. For you it might have a particular story line, but it's still a universal experience.

This isn't easy, but it's important that you allow yourself to experience whatever feeling or resistance arises in you. For example, I've found that often when we start working with emotions, a lot of people get really drowsy because they don't want to do this work. If you find that's true for you, you can just experience the drowsiness. You're moving toward a way to include emotional distress as your path of awakening.

Ken McLeod says that in order to truly experience something in the moment, there are two exits that you are choosing *not* to take. One, you are choosing not to act out by speaking, acting, or doing. Two, you are choosing not to repress anything. This is a standard meditation instruction that you can embody in the entirety of your life: do not act out and do not repress. See what happens if you don't do either of those things.

When you act out, the energy of your emotion goes into the action. In other words, you deflect the energy from the actual uncomfortable experience. I've found that when we do this, the energy comes back again and again and again. When you repress what happens, the energy that you're trying to move away from gets locked in your body, and it manifests as physical pain and illness.

Mingyur Rinpoche said that when you use emotions as a support and a friend rather than deflecting or repressing them, three things can happen. First, you turn your attention on the emotions, and as a result they disappear. Second, they might intensify. That's what often happens to me. Third, they remain the same. He says, "They disappear just as they are. They intensify just as they are. They stay the same just as they are." It's not like you're supposed to have a certain result. And we don't have to label these experiences as "good" or "bad."

One of the things that I and many other meditators have noticed is that, over time, when we stay with our emotions and breathe with them, the emotions can morph. Here is where we really develop the understanding that emotions are just energy; we see that emotions are simply energy that we attach our thoughts and stories to. Anger morphs into sadness, or it morphs into loneliness, or perhaps it even morphs into happiness. All of this can happen. And what I'd say when you begin to notice this is "Welcome to the lineage of meditators."

18

Drop the Story and Find the Feeling

As I've mentioned, one of the things that makes us get so lost in our emotions is that we attach our stories to them. I discovered quite a while back (and this was very liberating for me) that the escalation of emotions—where you're really in the river, swept away, losing all your perspective, totally carried away by loneliness and anger and despair—is fueled by the story line. Our emotions are like the stone thrown into the water, without the rings. An emotion, without the story, is immediate, sharp, and raw. The direct experience of the emotion creates no ripples. But with the story line, the ripples get bigger and bigger and go out farther and farther, and actually turn into waves and hurricane-velocity winds. The story line really churns things up.

You know how you might put on music in order to make yourself cry? You play a particular song and you just milk the sadness. Our story lines are like that, except we don't need music. We have our mind and our thoughts, and they can rev up the emotions. But if we use our emotions as the object of meditation, as our friend and support, it's like standing on the bank of the river and observing.

At Gampo Abbey, there are flagpoles out on the cliffs above the ocean. We keep experimenting with putting flags out there, because that's the point of flagpoles. Sometimes the weather is very calm, and we experience these lovely flags in the stillness of slight wind. Other times there are incredibly high winds, and the flags get shredded in a very short time. The image of the flagpole and the flag is a great one for working with thoughts and emotions, because the flagpole is steady and holds, and then the winds are whipping the flags all over the place, tearing them to shreds—that's usually our predicament. We *are* the flags, and the wind is just whipping us around. We're just whipped here and there and all over the place. And our emotions are escalating, our thoughts are all over the place. But using thoughts or emotions themselves as the object of meditation is experiencing life from the perspective of the flagpole. At Gampo Abbey, we never have to get new flagpoles. Even with hurricane-velocity winds, the flagpoles stay up on the cliffs.

exercise

FINDING THE FEELING

This exercise involves giving your friendly attention
to the experience or the felt sense of an emotion.
We're trying to get at a nonverbal experience.

Set your timer for twenty minutes. For a few
minutes, sit and get in touch with your breathing.
Just settle and breathe. Feel your breath going
in and out, and try to get a sense of spaciousness
in your breath.

When it feels like five minutes have passed, allow
yourself to bring up a memory that carries with it
a strong emotion. Perhaps a strong emotion that
feels more immediate has already surfaced.
If so, work with the first strong emotion that shows
up for you. Perhaps it isn't a so-called negative
emotion; perhaps it is joy.

First, what does the emotion feel like? Find its
texture and its color. Feel where it is located in your
body. Is it sharp, is it dull? Is it in your heart or in
your belly? You're looking for a felt answer.
It's like saying, "What does a toothache feel like?"
You don't have to describe it to yourself in words,
but you want to know that feeling.

If thoughts come up and distract you, just note
that and come back to experiencing. Come back
to just finding the feeling.

After a few minutes, what does the felt sense of the
emotion feel like? It's said that all experiences arise

and subside. Is that your experience? Thoughts can cause the energy of emotions to freeze or dwell for a long time. If we let go of the thoughts, the energy can move. Is that your experience?

If you're describing your felt sense of the emotion with a word, what does "pleasant" or "unpleasant" or "painful" or "tight" feel like? What does this word you've used to describe the emotion feel like? Maybe you're even using a word like "tingling" or "tense." What does that feel like?

Breathe in and out. Feeling it. Experiencing it. Resting in the experience.

If you're experiencing a strong emotion, you might want to breathe more deeply so that a sense of space and openness and friendliness can come in and support you. If you're feeling absolutely nothing at all, just a blank neutral state, breathe in and out and simply note: What does blank and neutral feel like? What does numb feel like?

If you're feeling resistance to doing this at all, experience that. You can keep asking yourself the question: What is this? Whether it's boredom, resistance, overwhelm, pain, pleasure, or drowsiness, try to get at the experience by asking yourself,

"What is this?" You're not looking for a verbal answer,
you're looking for an experience. What is this?

Now, really try to locate the strong emotion in
your body. A way to use emotions as a support,
as a friend, as a helper on the path of awakening,
is by using the way that the emotion is affecting
your body as your object of meditation. Rather
than using your whole body as the object, the
easiest thing is to just zero in on one part, to find
the feeling in the body. For instance, your body
temperature is rising, you're sweating, your palms
are moist, your stomach is in a knot, your brow is
furrowed. Choose one of those things. Mingyur
Rinpoche was once working with a student who
had severe depression, and he asked her what
it felt like. She said, "It feels like molten lava
throughout my whole body." He said, "OK, we're
going to use that feeling as the support, as the
friend for your awareness. Instead of focusing on
the whole body, just focus on your big toe."
So if you have an all-over feeling of some kind,
focus on that feeling in one part of your body,
if that's easier for you.

Sit with the feeling until your timer goes off.
When it rings, rest in the experience of whatever
came up for you. Sit in the home base of your

being, the vast spaciousness of your mind,
the open dimension of you.

After you practice with finding the feeling, it's very
common that the rumblings of the unpleasantness—
the clenched stomach or the sharpness in the
heart—are still there. The timer going off doesn't mean
that the feeling will go away. But there can be the
feeling of having a lot of space around the emotion.
We might feel less smothered by the emotion.

In this meditation exercise, we're training for real life.
Strong emotions will come in our life, and through
meditation we learn to give these emotions space so
that we can feel more settled when they do arise.

Part Four

WORKING WITH
SENSE PERCEPTIONS

*Buddha realized that true freedom lay not
in withdrawal from life but in a deeper
and more conscious engagement in its processes.*

—MINGYUR RINPOCHE

19

The Sense Perceptions

You can use anything as an object of meditation. You can use anything that's happening to you, whether it's the arising of thoughts or strong emotions or sense perceptions. Your object can be sheer delight for you, or it can be sheer misery. It's your choice.

For example, if you focus on a smell during your meditation, you might find yourself thinking, "That's a terrible smell! We shouldn't use that kind of incense" or "Oh, they're burning the oatmeal, and when I eat burned oatmeal I get terrible indigestion and I don't feel well for days." Once again you're off, and you're angry at the cook and you're packing your bags and you're leaving the meditation retreat. And it was all because of a smell!

Meditating on our sense perceptions—hearing, sight, feeling, tasting, and smelling—helps us to see that even the littlest thing can turn us toward full-blown internal warfare. Or a sense perception can just run us around in circles and keep us living in a fantasy world. They can show us how, basically, we cause our own suffering because we allow the most simple sense to bring back a memory that can then escalate difficult emotions.

On the other hand, they also are opportunities for us to enter pleasure, delight, and joy. The senses are so alive, and they can bring us right to the center of the present moment.

Meditating with the sense perceptions allows us to directly connect with the immediacy of our experience, which is our gateway to limitless experience, the vastness of this world. Again, these very same sense perceptions can keep you locked in. A sound can trigger a memory from a decade ago. A smell might make you think of how you need to clean out your refrigerator.

When we meditate with our sense perceptions, we interrupt the momentum of thoughts and come back to the sound, or the smell, or the feeling, or whatever sense you've chosen to place your attention on. If you can start to practice this way with every little thing throughout your day, you'll find that when challenges arise, you have tools for practice. You're used to interrupting the momentum of a trail of thoughts, such as "There's something wrong here that I have to solve," or "I'm a failure," or whatever the familiar story is. Through meditation, you're training in interrupting the momentum of the wandering mind and going right to the experience itself, which I have been calling the "felt sense" of the experience.

If you interrupt the momentum and abide with the felt experience of the moment, you find a doorway into the full possibility of awakening in this life. When we come into the immediacy of our experience, it is a nondualistic experience. In other words, by using our sense perceptions in meditation, we are coming into oneness with the sound or smell or whatever we are focusing on, rather than dividing ourselves in half.

For most people, the most accessible way to have a direct experience is to feel it physically. You feel it in your body, but there's also an atmosphere to the experience of a smell or a sound or a sight. Outside of the sensation, there's also an awareness of the sensation. Your ability to experience the atmosphere of a sensation will unfold over time, and slowly you can allow yourself to expand into that feeling as your object of meditation.

SOUND AS THE OBJECT OF MEDITATION

Often people cannot really have a direct sense perception of sound, because the sound invokes something in them that clouds their perception. It's the same with sight. You see something, and rather than being able to use it as an object of meditation, this particular sight has so many emotional associations that you become lost, and you can't really see. But you can keep coming back. You can just keep coming back. But this requires acknowledging that we bring a lot of baggage and conditioning along with this practice, which often causes us to get lost, and then we just have to keep coming back to the direct perception.

I have a story about an inmate in prison that communicates the complexity of our sense perceptions. I have heard the sounds in prison—it is deafening because people are in their cells, and the way they communicate with people on other sides and all the way up the tiers, is they yell. And they have developed the capacity to have a conversation with someone three tiers up, and they can actually hear each other going back and forth because they just tune out everything else and they just hear that. But for the untrained ear, it is just deafening because there are hundreds of these conversations going on, plus television sets, and a lot of noise, and a lot of just yelling—real yelling, very heated conversations.

So this man was sent a tape and it was a tape of the ocean sound. Someone found out he was doing some yoga, and they sent him this relaxation tape. He wore headphones to listen to it. He found it so relaxing—just listening to the ocean. He thought, I'm going to do these guys a favor. I'm going to broadcast the sounds of the ocean, and then everyone on the whole tier is going to chill out and relax."

He rigged up his tape so that everyone could hear the sounds of the ocean, and this simple action started a major panic attack. Someone said, "You hear that? What *is* that?" The prison was on the water, and so a few people heard the tape as the sound of the ocean rising. They started to panic, and then everyone was in a total panic. People were yelling things like, "I can see the water coming in, it's beginning to rise!" They were screaming at the guards, "Unlock our cells! Get us out of here! There's a flood coming!" So the sound had a totally different effect than the man expected!

I thought this story was so interesting. Maybe even a few of you panicked when you read about this man's experience, because at some point in your life you were in a flood, or the ocean rose and swept away your home when you were a little kid. For most people, the sound of the ocean is very soothing. But there was also this whole other meaning that was imputed on the sound; people attached a story to it, and it started a riot that escalated until literally everyone was involved in it.

This is a perfect example of what you're up against when you practice direct perception—the direct, unfiltered experience of anything. Our perceptions come with a lot of baggage. So that's why gently acknowledging that you're lost, and gently coming back, is important. And if your experience of a direct perception has triggered a deep-trauma reaction or panic, then be gentle with yourself and stop the practice altogether. Return to your practice when you feel ready to begin again.

exercise

SOUND AS THE OBJECT

When you sit for this practice, begin by checking your posture and getting as comfortable as you can. For this practice, try not to move. The intention behind not moving isn't to be harsh; it's meant to heighten your awareness so you don't spend the whole time wiggling around trying to get comfortable.

For a moment, sit and relax into your body, and notice whatever is going on with your body and your state of mind. No judgment. Just relax and notice your mood, the quality of your mind, the way your body is feeling.

Next, notice the sounds around you. Let sounds be the object of your meditation. You're doing shamatha practice here, where you take an object of meditation

and you let that be. Give all your attention to that
sound. When your attention wanders, simply
come back to the sound.

First, listen to distant sounds. You might hear closer
sounds, just a little rustling or something nearby.
Listen to distant sounds, and then if there are closer
sounds, listen to those, too.

There's no good or bad in this. Just relax and open
and listen. If thoughts take you away, realize that—
then just come back to listening.

Listen to the sound of the silence, which might
be punctuated by a sound in the distance
or something moving near you. Listen to the sound
of your heartbeat.

Sound doesn't have to be an interruption; it can
be the object of your meditation. You can include it,
and you can welcome it.

At the end of this practice, just relax. Take whatever
restful posture feels right for your body.

Sound is very interesting as the object of meditation.
Somehow the feeling of freshness, of big space
and complete relaxation, comes through. There is

something very expansive about listening to sound.
Allow sound in as the support, as your best friend
on this path of uncovering the natural awareness
of your mind.

SIGHT AS THE OBJECT OF MEDITATION

Working with sight is a little harder to stay with, and for that
reason you should practice with it. I recommend that you work
with three different eye gazes: really close down, a few feet in
front of you on the floor, and straight in front of you.

Normally, I instruct that the eyes are open, but the whole of
your attention doesn't always have to be on the specific object
that you're seeing. You can simply take in the sensation of what
you see—the space, the air, the wholeness of the field of vision
in front of you. You can also practice with the three different
eye gazes, and the object of meditation can be on whatever
your eyes fall on. You should stay with each gaze for just a
couple of minutes.

exercise

SIGHT AS THE OBJECT

For the first eye gaze, the gaze can be close down.
When your eyes fall downward, what do you see? Let

that become your object of meditation. Keep looking at it. When the mind wanders off, just come back.

For the next gaze, use your typical eye gaze, which is about four to six feet in front of you. Again, the object of meditation is whatever your eyes see.

Finally, look straight ahead, and it's the same—you'll just look out and maybe you take one aspect of what you see and you just let that be the object of your meditation. You are using something visual as a shamatha object.

For each gaze, just look. Not saying good or bad, right or wrong, pretty or ugly. Just look.

If your eyes do funny things, look at that and don't get distracted. Or if you do get distracted, come back to looking at whatever's happening there. When you use the visual consciousness, you often do have visual illusions, like seeing light and squiggles and little flashes of things. That's fine. It's not good or bad; you can just include that. And if nothing happens, that's fine, too.

If your attention wanders, just notice that—thinking—very gentle. Just let it go, let it dissolve, and come back to looking. If something you see starts a chain reaction of thought, when you realize that, just touch it lightly: "thinking . . . thinking." Come back to just looking. Let it be very light, relaxed, and nonjudgmental.

When you've come to the end of this meditation, let yourself relax.

SENSATION AS THE OBJECT OF MEDITATION

It is always quite enlivening to meditate on sensation or feeling consciousness, or what I sometimes call touch consciousness. When you first sit down, begin by going over your posture, tuning in to where you're at in terms of your body and your mood and your state of mind. We are training ourselves to do this without a judgmental attitude. Really bring as much of that spaciousness and relaxation—lightness, gentleness, kindness, and sense of delight—into this as you can. Just notice that you go off with sheer delight. And come back with sheer delight.

exercise

SENSATION AS THE OBJECT

First, experience the sensation of your bottom touching the cushion. Let that feeling, that sensation, be the object of your meditation. You don't even have to say "painful," or "relaxed," or anything at all. Just see if you can feel it; have a direct experience of the sensation of your bottom touching the cushion. Try not to think about your bottom touching the floor, just feel the sensation—a direct experience of the sensation; a direct, nonverbal experiencing of the sensation.

Next, feel your hands—the sensation of your hands touching your legs. Feel whatever your hands are touching—a direct sensation of that; a direct, felt experience; an experiencing of the sensation of your hands touching.

If you have trouble feeling that sensation, you can move the hands ever so slightly. Or you can just move one finger so you have an experience of sensation, a direct awareness of sensation.

If you haven't already done so, take your hands and place them on your thighs palms down. Can you feel the pulse in your hands, or any tingling in your hands? Put your full attention on your hands. See if you can feel the pulse or a tingling in your hands—a direct, nonverbal experience.

Can you feel anything in your arms?
Can you feel the pulse in your arms, or a

tingling or any sensation at all in your arms?
Feel your hands and your arms.

Can you feel the pulse or tingling or any
sensation at all in your stomach or in your chest?
What is the sensation there?

What's it like feeling the energy in your body?
In your hands, your arms, your stomach,
and your chest? Can you feel something there,
some sensation inside the body?

People often tense in their belly. Right now see
if there's a sensation of holding or tightness
in the belly, and if there is, relax that and feel
that sensation of tightening and relaxing. If it's
tight, just see if you can relax it and just feel that
sensation of relaxing the lower belly—soft belly.
Can you feel the belly or the abdomen rising and
falling as you breathe? Not watching it or thinking
about it, but feeling it. Feel the sensation of the
breath moving in and out. Sometimes the breath
will be deep, and sometimes the breath will be
shallow. Whatever it is, just experience that. Just
experience the breath as it is right now, moving in
and out of your body, through your nose, through
your mouth. Just experience the breath moving
in and out of your body.

The breath going in and out is your usual object of meditation; see if you can have a direct experience of this. It's not concentration, it's not grasping, it's not forcing. It's very natural, open awareness to experiencing the breath going in and out; it's being with the breath going in and out. Trungpa Rinpoche used to say, "Be with the breath. Be one with the breath going in and out."

Stay very relaxed, and if you have been following after the momentum of the thoughts, just kindly note that as "thinking." Then come back again to the breath going in and out; experience being with the breath, allowing the breath as it goes in and out.

You can direct your attention to any pain, tightness, or discomfort in the body. If there's any pain, discomfort, or tightness, let that be the object of your meditation. Just feeling, experiencing, giving your light but fully compassionate attention to that spot of pain, discomfort, or tightness. Let that be the object of your meditation. Not thinking about it, just feeling the sensation of what we call pain, tightness, or discomfort. Place your attention directly on that spot or that area, and experience the sensation . . . not "my pain," or "me in pain," but just the sensation.

I have a friend who discovered the most helpful thing. She absolutely found it impossible to use the breath as the object of her meditation, and generally when you're given meditation instruction, that's the most common suggestion: to place your light awareness on the breath. So, someone introduced her to using sense perceptions as support, and she found that so much more helpful. To actually feel, for example, her hands, her hands on her knees, her thighs and knees, her feet on the floor, or her buttocks sitting on the cushion, allowed her to really open to what was actually meant by using an object as the support for meditation. Somehow her battles with bad asthma made it very hard for her to focus on her breath, but when she started working with touch, she was really able to drop in to her meditation practice. This was her entrance into being able to use any object as support for her meditation.

TASTE AS THE OBJECT OF MEDITATION

Taste, or eating, is always wonderful to use as an ally for awakening. Often in retreats people will start with an eating exercise. Thich Nhat Hanh teaches this, as do other spiritual teachers. For example, he will encourage you to try eating a section of an orange with your full attention on the taste and texture. When people do this, one of the interesting points they note is how tricky it can be to distinguish between really tasting—having a direct experience of the taste—and thinking about taste.

Chocolate is a fantastic example of this. We have so many thoughts around chocolate! Perhaps you consider it to be something forbidden that you rarely let yourself eat because you've been trying to lose weight, and someone very malicious gave you a beautiful, little box with three truffles in it. Or maybe you hold this concept of the pleasure it's going to give you. And maybe the first bite is a really direct experience because you haven't tasted chocolate for a long time and you love it. Then you get to truffle number two, and the spiral of everything you impute or invest chocolate with begins. At this point, you've lost the direct experience.

One of the things that people often say to me is: "Working with sense perceptions seems like too much for me because if anything can be the object of meditation, then I feel like I'm all over the place and I'm constantly swept away, even though I know that's not the point." In response, I realize that this person hasn't fully registered the instruction on just coming back—just coming back, just coming back. I want to reemphasize this, because when you're working with taste, after you take the first bite and move on to the second, you can actually end up wandering in that second moment—it is so easy to drift.

The first second is always fresh. Trungpa Rinpoche used to refer to this as "First thought, best thought"—even though in this case there's no thought, but the sensation of taste. First thought is the fresh moment. If someone says to me, "Ani Pema," and I turn, there's the fresh moment. Then comes the second moment, the concept of the person or the expectation of what they're going to say, or the "Oh no, I don't want to talk to them," or "Oh joy, it's the person I've been longing to see." First moment, best moment. Our life is full of these completely fresh moments, completely fresh tastes.

exercise

TASTE AS THE OBJECT

The basic instruction for working with taste is simply to stay with the taste. When you take a bite of food (and I recommend you practice with a simple taste—food— perhaps it is a strawberry, or a raisin), allow yourself to deepen into the taste—just experience the taste. Not the action of chewing. Not the texture of the food. Simply the sensation of the taste.

When you notice that you've wandered off, just come back. If you move into thoughts, it's not bad, and it's not a mistake. Just simply return to awareness of the taste. The training is being fully present to the taste. Say to yourself, "I can use this taste to train myself in being present. I don't have to be swept away. I don't have to drown in my emotions, or persecute myself with thoughts. I don't have to escalate stress or fear. I can stop and use this one taste as a support for stabilizing the mind, for staying present, for returning to fresh, direct experience."

Mingyur Rinpoche has written about being a participant in a Mind and Life Institute experiment that was instigated by

His Holiness the Dalai Lama. Meditators were put into fMRI machines so researchers could see on a graph what happens in the minds of dedicated meditators. The scientists discovered that when you do the habitual thing, when your mind is on automatic pilot and you're swept away, lost in thought, or escalating into your emotions, it's registered in the brain as deep grooves. They're like habit-grooves, and they get deeper every time you do the same thing. This is the actual neurological explanation for why it's so hard to break a habit: it's because we keep making the groove deeper and deeper.

However, when you realize you've been thinking, when you realize you've been wandering, when you realize you've been lost in thought and suddenly there's that gap, this recognition opens up a new neurological pathway. It's like predisposing yourself to seeing the world with fresh eyes, predisposing yourself to tuning in to the natural spaciousness, freshness, and openness of your being and the world. And every time you place your mind on the object of a sense perception and you're there, it's the same thing: it opens up a new pathway.

So anytime during your life, instead of reinforcing the old patterns that are going to make it harder and harder for you to not just keep on automatic pilot—reinforcing the causes of suffering in your life—you can predispose yourself to a fresh way of seeing, which on the fMRI graphs appears as unblocking or opening new neurological pathways. In other words, you're creating your future here. The choices you make are creating your next moment, your next hour, your next day, your next month, your next year. Your whole lifetime is being determined moment by moment by the choices you make. I've found that working with the sense perceptions is a quite effective and sometimes delightful way of training yourself so that these new grooves can form.

20

THE INTERCONNECTION
OF ALL PERCEPTIONS

You can't really separate out what happens in your body, your thoughts, and your emotions from one another. And it is the same with your sense perceptions. They're all intertwined. You hear a certain piece of music or a certain sound, and then a strong emotion arises. Suddenly, you have a visual memory and a strong storyline arises and it's all a conglomerate. So rather than allowing the conglomerate experience to become overwhelming or confusing, you can just take any part of it—any part of it—and use that as the support for your meditation.

Coming from the point of view of space and the infinite potential of space, we see that everything and anything can occur and does occur. Sights, sounds, emotions—there's a lot going on. It's not just a big space void, with nothing happening, but a dynamic interplay of thoughts, emotions, and perceptions that are happening all the time. We use what's happening as a friend, as an ally on this path of uncovering the fundamental freshness, openness, and wakefulness of our mind.

There is a deep interdependence between everything we experience. For example, we call something "anger," but it has a physical component, it has a visual component, it has a story line, and it has a texture and color. Nothing is as solid as it seems. We see that what we call "anger" is very fluid. And the anger moves; it changes, if we stay with it. If we use the energy of the anger as our object of meditation, it inevitably points us to impermanence and change, to realizing that transiency is the true nature of reality. If you want to experience transiency or dynamic flow or impermanence firsthand, practice being present with one thing—the breath, a sound, an emotion. That's the way to do it.

It is said that all deep satisfaction, all happiness, all spiritual growth, all feeling of being alive and engaged in the world happens in this realm of dynamic flow when we connect with the fluid, changing flow of things. In some way, all of us are at least five-minute fundamentalists. In other words, where we fix it, we freeze it. Rather than being with the flow, we have a fixed view of somebody else: a fixed view of a brother or a partner, a fixed view of ourselves, a fixed view of a situation. There's so much clunkiness in the whole thing. If you think about it, fixing and freezing is so boring compared to the real morphing quality of things.

It might take a lot of persuasion for me to convince you that your mother is not the fixed identity you hold her to be, because every time you think of your mother, she is nothing other than how you've always seen her. "Whenever I do this, she does that; and then she says this, and these are her views," and so on. Then one day, you happen to meet an old friend of your mother's, and it's very interesting: when the old friend talks about your mother, it sounds like a completely different person. "I love your mom's sense of humor. She's so lighthearted and funny!" Of course, the fact that your mother has also frozen *you* doesn't help the situation! Whether it's your mother, partner, sister, boss, whoever it is, it is usually in intimacy that we most freeze people, but we also do it to whole racial groups, to whole cultural groups, to whole religions, to politicians who hold certain political beliefs—we tend toward getting comfort out of being fundamentalists. Which is when we say: it's like this. But all you have to do is this practice of meditation, of simply being present to your experience, whatever occurs, letting it be your friend and support, your ally for awakening—just coming back, coming back, being here, touching in, fully present as much as you possibly can be—present to going off, present to coming back—and you immediately see that nothing is fixed. Nothing is solid except these fabrications created by your mind: these imaginary, fixed identities of yourself and others, or situations, or places.

And as for the idea that someone in your life has a fixed idea of you, keep meditating. You'll be surprised. When something changes from your side and you see that how your emotional responses are operating, then something changes in the dynamic between you and the other person. Something new can be revealed.

Locking into a fixed way of seeing things gives us a sense of certainty and security—but it's false security, it's false certainty, and ultimately it's not satisfying. The satisfaction that we seek comes from recognizing the inevitable flux and flow and morphing and changing of things, and it comes from the ability to see the organic, true nature of whatever is arising in the present.

Part Five

OPENING YOUR HEART TO INCLUDE EVERYTHING

The experience of a sad and tender heart is what gives birth to fearlessness. Conventionally, being fearless means that you are not afraid or that, if someone hits you, you will hit him back. But we aren't talking about that street-fighter level of fearlessness. Real fearlessness is the product of tenderness. It comes from letting the world tickle your heart, your raw heart. You are willing to open up, without resistance or shyness, and face the world.

—CHÖGYAM TRUNGPA RINPOCHE

21

GIVING UP THE STRUGGLE

One of the many boons of meditation is that it helps us take an interest in our life in a way that is curious and expansive, rather than seeing life's complexities as a constant struggle. By "struggle," I mean not wanting life to be the way it is. This is really common. Exploring this in my own experience, I've found that we aren't just constantly rejecting our experiences in life—very often we reject the whole thing all the time!

The symptom that shows us this is true is that our minds are always elsewhere. We're thinking about dinner tomorrow or a conversation from a year ago. We're thinking about our to-do list or how we wish we had said this, that, and the other thing in yesterday's conversation. Rejecting our life isn't always about carrying a big story line such as "I hate this" or "This relationship or this job or this car isn't working for me." In many cases, we can even be eating a whole box of chocolates with the idea that we are doing the most pleasurable thing in the world, but the fact is that we rarely allow ourselves to eat even one bite of chocolate and be fully present for it.

The mind—the monkey mind, the wild mind—wanders. Yet in this space of open awareness that we cultivate on the meditation cushion, whatever arises becomes our support for training in being present. In order to get to this place of nonstruggling, we allow every single thing that occurs in our practice and in our life to be a support for being present. This takes an enormous shift in attitude. Rather than seeing everything as a problem, or an obstacle to being happy, or even as an obstacle to meditation and being present ("I could be present if it wasn't so noisy here," or "I could be present if I didn't have so much pain in my back"), we can see it as a teacher that is showing us something we need to know.

Everything is support in our awakening. We've been conditioned to kvetch, kvetch, kvetch. Blame, blame, blame. One of the major ways that we don't stay present is blaming. We blame ourselves; we blame other people. I often see students blaming the outer circumstances or blaming their own bodies and minds for why they can't be present. Consider that what needs your attention and consideration is your own mind, and how you view these outer circumstances. You can befriend your circumstances; you can have compassion for your circumstances and for yourself. What happens when you do that?

I recently heard contentment defined as "knowing that everything you need is contained in this present moment." Dissatisfaction and discontent are like a hum in the background that distracts us from accepting our life and the present moment. If we deeply allow whatever arises, we finally can touch, smell, taste, hear, and feel what's really happening.

When we refrain from pushing against our experiences, we move away from the labels of "yes" and "no," "good" and "bad," "acceptable" and "nonacceptable." This is a very important point. This is what allows us to become fully engaged in life. You can't leave out what you label "bad" and still expect to feel the full range of what you might label "good." In other words, if you wall yourself off from some experiences, you will inevitably be building walls against what might be good. Meditation training reminds us to always come back to our direct experience, just as it is.

Life, or postmeditation, has a tendency to introduce many things and many obstacles that can tie us up in a knot. As your meditation closes, when the timer goes off and you rest in open awareness, let things be as they are. And then, usually very quickly, you can rest. But often at this moment the thoughts come in; sometimes they even rush back in. Before you know it, you're getting all tied up in a knot. When something happens, you don't have to lay on top of it the label "wrong" or "terrible" or anything like that—you could just use whatever is arising as the object of meditation. Meditation is total nonstruggle with what arises. Thoughts just as they are, emotions just as they are, sights just as they are, sounds just as they are—everything just as it is without anything added.

I was watching a video of Mingyur Rinpoche recently, and he said that mind is like space—vast, limitless space—and in that space anything and everything arises: sights, sounds, smells, tastes, thoughts, emotions, body pain, body pleasure. Everything arises in that space, and it's no different than galaxies and planets and stars arising in space. And he said, "Space doesn't say, 'I like this galaxy, but I don't like that galaxy.'" All stars, all thoughts, pass on at some point. Let your experiences pass through like stars in the vast sky of your mind. Nothing has to be too big of a problem.

Not struggling against what arises in your life is an act of friendliness. It allows you to fully engage in your life. It allows you to live wholeheartedly.

exercise

ATTENTION TO A SIMPLE ACTIVITY AS MEDITATION

Life presents all kinds of experiences that introduce potential struggle into our life. One way that you can train in meeting experiences with full presence, wholeheartedly, is by using a simple activity as the object of your meditation. We're training in the process of waking up. We can place the mind on a simple activity and choose to stay with it rather than struggle against it by letting our minds wander elsewhere.

We are offered many simple activities every day— repetitive and simple. Select one that feels pretty routine and basic for you. Eating is a good one. Every day you put food on your fork or spoon, bring the food into your mouth, chew it, and put the fork or spoon down. Choose any activity that doesn't require any thinking, or very little thinking, and choose something that you do over and over again. It could be touching computer keys, folding your clothes, making your child's lunch for school. Our days are filled with such activities. Meditation includes training yourself in being fully present with brushing your teeth or washing the dishes or eating breakfast or breathing or walking. We're training in the process of waking up.

For a series of days, focus on being more present when you partake in the activity you selected. When your attention lapses, simply bring it back to the felt experience of the activity. Coming back to the breath is no more of a big deal than coming back to your toothbrush. When you're brushing your teeth, decide as you're about to put the toothpaste on the brush that this is a meditation. Make brushing your teeth a little bit of a ritual. It's an activity that has a beginning and an end, so say to yourself: "This is going to be a meditation period, and my intention is to stay present as I'm brushing my teeth. When my attention wanders, I'm going to bring it back to brushing my teeth."

Needless to say, one doesn't need to be so hard on oneself when one's mind wanders off from brushing

the teeth. Don't struggle too much. Just come back.
Brush your teeth with a sense of humor, or a sense
of lightness. Just come back.

With meditation practice, slowly over time we find
that we are more and more able to stay present in
everything we do. We can even do it when we're
having a conversation: we stay mindful and present
to the person speaking to us, rather than wandering
off to what we need to add to our shopping list.

After a while, you don't even think about an object of
meditation. There's just the continual coming back,
and a more and more continuous sense of presence.
And when that happens, you know that it's happened.
Usually it happens in little blips and blurps, but it's
quite dramatic when you realize that you've never
been present in your whole life before, and suddenly
there's this simple experience of being fully here.
It can happen out of the blue one day when you're
meditating, or it can happen when you're washing
a dish. The sense that you are just being present
is so simple and so gorgeously alive.
It is a big breakthrough.

22

THE SEVEN DELIGHTS

As people who wish to attain enlightenment, or simply feel more settled in our life, we must be willing to work with even the most difficult circumstances. I've seen people meditating wholeheartedly for years and years and years—people who have experienced the nature of their mind, people who have experienced stillness and calm—but as soon as a relationship goes bad or they get fired from a job or they find out they have a serious illness or that someone they love is sick, they collapse. It's as if they never meditated a day in their life, and they are completely taken away into anger or despair or a dark depression.

When something strong and scary comes up, we don't want to "go there." We go into automatic pilot and we do everything we can to struggle against what is happening. Then we tend to fixate on the despair and the anger. It's like we've lost the meditation bandwidth completely; we've lost our way on the path. There's a path quality to your meditation practice, and the way becomes much less clear when you hit the toughest points.

I call these moments the "seven delights." Believe it or not, sometimes these tough moments are the very things that teach us the most; sometimes they are the very things that open us up to life and to connection with others.

On retreats, sometimes we read through a text about the seven delights that reminds us how aching emotions and harsh thoughts can be the perfect teacher for us on our path. In this wonderful song about using difficult circumstances as path, which was written by Gotsampa, there is a number that refers to one of the difficulties in life that can be viewed as a delight in our awakening. The term *kleshas* in the song refers to the emotional states that tend to hook us or disturb us the most.

When thoughts that there is something, perceived
    and a perceiver,
Lure my mind away and distract,
I don't close my senses' gateways to meditate
    without them
But plunge straight into their essential point.
They're like clouds in the sky; there's this shimmer
    where they fly.
Thoughts that rise (1), for me sheer delight!

When kleshas get me going, and their heat has got
    me burning,
I try no antidote to set them right.
Like an alchemistic potion turning metal into gold,
What lies in kleshas' power to bestow
Is bliss without contagion, completely undefiled.
Kleshas coming up (2), sheer delight!

When I'm plagued by godlike forces or
    demonic interference,
I do not drive them out with rites and spells.
The thing to chase away is egoistic thinking,
Built up on the idea of a self.
This will turn the ranks of *maras* into your own
    special forces.
When obstacles arise (3), sheer delight!

When *samsara* with its anguish has me writhing
    in its torments,
Instead of wallowing in misery,
I take the greater burden down the greater path
    to travel
And let compassion set me up
To take upon myself the sufferings of others.
When karmic consequences bloom (4), delight!

When my body has succumbed to the attacks
    of painful illness,
I do not count on medical relief,
But take that very illness as a path and by its power
Remove the obscurations blocking me,
And use it to encourage the qualities worthwhile.
When illness rears its head (5), sheer delight!

When it's time to leave this body, this illusionary tangle,
Don't cause yourself anxiety and grief.

The thing that you should train in and clear up
    for yourself—
There's no such thing as dying to be done.
It's just clear light, the mother and child clear
    light uniting,
When mind forsakes the body (6), sheer delight!

When the whole thing's just not working, everything's
    lined up against you,
Don't try to find some way to change it all.
Here the point to make your practice is reverse the
    way you see it.
Don't try to make it stop or to improve.
Adverse conditions happen (7); when they do
    it's so delightful.

They make a little song of sheer delight!

Everything in your life—every moment, every struggle—is the path. Everything is an opportunity for awakening. Without practicing this way, you lose the extraordinary opportunity to learn from your very own being. This is why I call these gigantic hiccups in life "delights."

We all have difficult emotions and difficult events in our life, both now and in the past. For instance, no matter how many retreats I do, no matter how many sitting periods I take part in, I have a reoccurring pattern that happens: I always have to go through a period of painful memories about things I regret from the period when my children were young. This always comes up, and it's always accompanied by deep sadness. Certain things carry a great deal of energy along with them. And so, when we say "including" or "experiencing" our emotional distress, I mean we include *all* of it.

Sometimes we're sitting with a lot of energy. From the outsider's perspective, you are just sitting there. Nothing is happening. But so much is happening! It's just nonverbal. Behind the words and stories of what is happening in our lives there's this very powerful energy—the energy of sadness; the energy of anger; the energy of craving, lusting, needing; the energy of loneliness; the energy of being left out. It feels as though it is going to completely bowl you over. And when it is really hard, like the loss of a loved one, it might feel like it could even kill you.

In Dilgo Khyentse Rinpoche's text *The Heart Treasure of the Enlightened Ones,* there's a beautiful instruction that says: "Don't follow after the object of hatred, look at the angry mind. Anger liberated by itself as it arises is mirrorlike wisdom." And then: "Don't chase after the object of pride, look at the grasping mind. Self-importance liberated by itself as it arises is the wisdom of equanimity." And: "Don't hanker after the object of desire, look at the craving mind." He goes through all the mental states that cloud the mind in this way, and he's basically saying, "They're not a problem if you will give these tendencies your attention."

The first line of the seven delights text says: "When thoughts that there is something, perceived and a perceiver."

Here Gotsampa means that with all thoughts, we are forced to see the world, or the situation, in terms of self and other. This is basically what all thoughts are about, right? *I* am thinking about *that;* "me" and "it." It's hard to have a thought that isn't based on that. See if you can have a thought that doesn't have a perceived and a perceiver. It is virtually impossible!

Gotsampa goes on to say: "[When those thoughts] lure my mind away and distract." Usually in meditation you think, "Oh my gosh, my mind has been lured away and distracted!" Then you kick the thought in the head by saying to yourself, "I am that thought; I am bad to have done this; my meditation is a wreck." So the sage reminds us that instead, he "plunge[s] straight into their essential point." He basically says that he doesn't try to block the thoughts; he doesn't try to meditate without the thoughts. He plunges right into them, right into the essential point, which is that, "[These thoughts are] like clouds in the sky; there's this shimmer where they fly." It's a beautiful line: "They're like clouds in the sky; there's this shimmer where they fly. / Thoughts that rise, for me sheer delight." I love this poem because it presents a view that can bring such joy into your life. He's saying, "Adverse conditions happen, and when they do it's so delightful. They make a little song of sheer delight." They are delight because they allow us to awaken to the fresh truth of our life. Even the hardest things allow us to awaken to the moment.

In another verse, Gotsampa says: "When the kleshas get me going, and their heat has got me burning." Gotsampa knew what a klesha felt like, yet he doesn't say, "Do anything you can to squelch the emotion." Instead he says: "Like an alchemistic potion, turning metal into gold / What lies in klesha's power to bestow / Is bliss without contagion, completely undefiled. / Kleshas coming up, sheer delight!" This is a very profound teaching, and it's actually what we're doing when we meditate through the most adverse conditions. We are welcoming the view that the things which we think are wrecking our life—like our thoughts and our emotions, or illness and death—are actually gifts for our transformation. He says: "Here the point to make your practice is reverse the way you see it." Reverse the way you see the kleshas. You could see them as a cloud in the sky and say, "No big deal," and with the attitude of sheer delight, let them go.

The seven delights introduce the idea that nothing is fundamentally a problem, except our identification with it. We have a very strong identity with our thoughts and emotions and the events in our life. We can't kid ourselves about that. Whether life presents us with a pleasant sound or an unpleasant sound, a pleasant smell or an unpleasant smell, a pleasant thought or an unpleasant thought, it's sheer delight because instead of identifying with the experience, we simply touch it and let it go.

We can let go of even the most intense fears that we carry. Our fears can be very, very mighty! For example, at times we are confronted with the fear of death. This fear can come from waiting for results about a medical test or from a close call in a car accident. There are so many ways we come up against our mortality. But fear of death is yet another thing that we can train with, in small moments, because the fear of death is really a fear of groundlessness, of having nothing to hold on to, of having no certainty about what will come to pass in our life. I don't mean for this to be trite or superficial. Through many years of working with the fear of death myself and talking with a lot of other people about it, I've found that if you train in moving toward the impermanent, transient nature of things, then you're training in short-circuiting the fear of groundlessness, or the fear of death.

I've found that the fear of the unknown is a sort of knee-jerk reaction. You don't need to feed it with a story line. Rather, you can stay present with the quaky, trembly feeling. It's the same as the instruction for working with emotions. Allow yourself to be with the energy of the fear of death. Place your awareness on the fear. There can be tension in your stomach, your thoughts can be going wild, and yet you can just focus on the quality and texture of fear itself. Watch how your experience of this fear begins to morph and change, to intensify and release.

There are a lot of views about what happens when we die. Every world religion has an opinion on this subject. But we don't really know, do we? Each moment is also unknown, and the path of awakening is about not rejecting what arises but instead delighting in the aliveness of everything that shows up.

23

THE BEARABLE
LIGHTNESS OF BEING

Meditation teaches us how to let go. It's actually a very important aspect of friendliness, which is that you train again and again in not making things such a big deal. When you have pain in your body, when all sorts of thoughts are going through your mind, you train again and again in acknowledging them openheartedly and open-mindedly, but not making them such a big deal.

Generally speaking, the human species does make things a very big deal. Our problems are a big deal for us. So we need to make space for an attitude of honoring things completely and at the same time not making them a big deal. It's a paradoxical idea, but holding these two attitudes simultaneously is the source of enormous joy: we hold a sense of respect toward all things, along with the ability to let go. So it's about not belittling things, but on the other hand not fanning the fire until you have your own private World War III.

Keeping these ideas in balance allows us to feel less crowded and claustrophobic. In Buddhist terms, the space that opens here is referred to as *shunyata,* or "emptiness." But there's nothing nihilistic about this emptiness. It's basically just a feeling of lightness. There is movie entitled *The Unbearable Lightness of Being,* but I prefer to see life from the view of the Bearable Lightness of Being.

When you begin to see life from the point of view that everything is spontaneously arising and that things aren't "coming at you" or "trying to attack you," in any given moment you will likely experience more space and more room to relax into. Your stomach, which is in a knot, can just relax. The back of your neck, which is all tensed up, can just relax. Your mind, which is spinning and spinning like one of those little bears that you wind up so it walks across the floor, can just relax. So shunyata refers to the fact that we actually have a seed of spaciousness, of freshness, openness, relaxation, in us.

Sometimes the word *shunyata* has been translated as the "open dimension of our being." The most popular definition is "emptiness," which sounds like a big hole that somebody pushes you into, kicking and screaming: "No, no! Not emptiness!" Sometimes people experience this openness as boredom. Sometimes it's experienced as stillness. Sometimes it's experienced as a gap in your thinking and your worrying and your all-caught-up-ness.

I experiment with shunyata a lot. When I'm by myself and no one's talking to me, when I'm simply going for a walk or looking out the window or meditating, I experiment with letting the thoughts go and just seeing what's there when they go. This is actually the essence of mindfulness practice. You keep coming back to the immediacy of your experience, and then when the thoughts start coming up, thoughts like, *bad, good, should, shouldn't, me, jerk, you, jerk,* you let those thoughts go, and you come back again to the immediacy of your experience. This is how we can experiment with shunyata, how we can experiment with the open, boundless dimension of being.

24

BELIEFS

There was a yoga teacher in India in the twelfth century named Saraha, and he said (to loosely paraphrase him): "Those who believe in existence as solid are stupid. Those who believe that everything is empty are even more stupid." He was referring to any beliefs that limit our experience and cause us to be unable to perceive what's in front of our eyes and nose. Beliefs that we hold so strongly and so dearly that we're willing to fight for them, beliefs that blind us and make us deaf.

I've found that one of the biggest struggles arising from meditation practice is when it asks us to examine our belief systems. A lot of meditation practice is about beginning to find those moments when you get stubborn and cannot let go. You meet those moments when you get righteously indignant, and you see that all you can do is either harden and wall yourself off from the world further, or you can soften, let go, and relax. In other words, the only way at all that a practitioner—or a human being—knows that they are still holding tight to beliefs or a way of seeing the world is when they get upset, when they get heated, when they find themselves quarreling with someone about anything because they want it their way. This "You're wrong and I'm right" thinking keeps us in a certain kind of prison.

This is the juice of the spiritual path: when you begin to get stubborn and opinionated and righteously indignant, when you get hot under the collar and panicked that things are not going to go your way. That's the only way you know that you're making yourself unhappy, and it's like a big bell going off. That's the time to let the thoughts go, and to train in opening your heart and opening your mind. It all comes down to the meditation instruction of letting go.

This righteous indignation, this panic that someone is going to do it wrong, this dogma you feel that the world will go under if things don't go your way, is actually a form of aggression. This is true even if the belief is so-called good; for instance, the belief that we need to clean up pollution in the rivers. When we hold on tightly to a certain way of seeing things, we're poisoning ourselves, and it doesn't bring any happiness to ourselves or to anyone else. Our good views don't produce good results because they're coming from such panic, such aggression, and such determination to have it our way. And there's so much sense of an enemy.

All our beliefs are based on thoughts, and the energy of those thoughts make us emotional, even hysterical. So in meditation, we get to have an in-depth, earnest discussion with ourselves. A *really* serious talk. In this respect, well-being and making peace with ourselves has a lot to do with the quality of space we find in meditation, which is called shunyata, or emptiness. This open space reminds us to "lighten up."

As I've said, the more you work wholeheartedly with this kind of practice, one of the first things you're going to discover is that you don't want to lighten up. You want to have it your way. I once asked a Tibetan teacher, a wild yogi and a wonderful person, about my tendency to get sleepy during practice. I said, "I get drowsy all the time, and I think it's more than just needing a good night's rest. I'm actually sort of habitually nodding out and drowsy, kind of clouded. What can I do?"

And he said, "You should just say *POT!*"

I just started laughing! I knew it would work. After he said that, I didn't feel drowsy in my practice for some time. But sure enough, habitual patterns returned, and there I was supposedly meditating, and I would get very drowsy and I'd want to lie down. Then I would remember what he said about how I could say *POT!* Then I said, "I don't want to say *POT!* I want to lie down!" And so I would lie down. But I couldn't rest very well, because I caught myself in this trick. The pleasure of lying down was somewhat interrupted by my insight into what was going on.

I realized that this is what we're all up against, every single one of us. Even if someone said, "All you have to do is eat this little pill, and your pain will go away," you'll find that you don't want to. You want to go to sleep. Or you want to prove them wrong. Or you want to have it turn out your way. You don't want to eat the pill or say *POT!* or meditate or soften, or any of that stuff. You want it your way.

Our beliefs are an excellent opportunity to have a good laugh about the human condition, and to remind ourselves how we are all in this together. How tightly we hold on to our beliefs reminds us of what we're all up against. We could get in the habit of going back to the out-breath, which is the same as coming back to the freshness of the moment. This is very difficult when the moment is pregnant with a lot of energy—because very often your beliefs lock you down into angry thoughts; jealous thoughts; very desperately lonely, sad thoughts; addictive thoughts; craving, wanting thoughts. When you look at your beliefs in meditation, you often find yourself sitting in a highly charged atmosphere. Get used to sitting there, breathing into it, rather than trying to escape. Pain can arise in space. Depression and fear can arise in space. We can make the space bigger so that we can let whatever arises be there because we put space around it. We put some softness and warmth around it.

And bring as much honesty as you can to your practice. When you feel any kind of firmness of mind, keep asking questions. Ask and ask questions. Get curious, and open yourself to the space of meditation. This is how the world speaks to you.

25

RELAXING WITH
GROUNDLESSNESS

Whether we're studying Buddhism or doing Buddhist practice, we should realize that the essence of the practice is discovering how we misperceive reality. We actually have a misperception of reality. And what we're doing through meditation is training in being able to perceive reality correctly.

Enlightenment—full enlightenment—is perceiving reality with an open, unfixated mind, even in the most difficult circumstances. It's nothing more than that, actually. You and I have had experiences of this open, unfixated mind. Think of a time when you have felt shock or surprise; at a time of awe or wonder we experience it. It's usually in small moments, and we might not even notice it, but everyone experiences this open, so-called enlightened mind. If we were completely awake, this would be our constant perception of reality. It's helpful to realize that this open, unfettered mind has many names, but let's use the term "buddha nature."

You could say it's as if we are in a box with a tiny little slit. We perceive reality out of that little slit, and we think that's how life is. And then as we meditate—particularly if we train in the way that I'm suggesting—if we train in gentleness, and if we train in letting go, if we bring relaxation as well as faithfulness to the technique into the equation; if we work with open eyes and with being awake and present, and if we train that way moment after moment in our life—what begins to happen is that the crack begins to get bigger, and it's as if we perceive more. We develop a wider and more tolerant perspective.

It might just be that we notice that we're sometimes awake and we're sometimes asleep; or we notice that our mind goes off, and our mind comes back. We begin to notice—the first big discovery, of course—that we think so, so much. We begin to develop what's called *prajna*, or "clear wisdom." With this clear wisdom, we are likely to feel a growing sense of confidence that we can handle more, that we can even love more. Perhaps there are times when we are able to climb out of the box altogether. But believe me, if that happened too soon, we would freak out. Usually we're not ready to perceive out of the box right away. But we move in that direction. We are becoming more and more relaxed with uncertainty, more and more relaxed with groundlessness, more and more relaxed with not having walls around us to keep us protected in a little box or cocoon.

Enlightenment isn't about going someplace else or attaining something that we don't have right now. Enlightenment is when the blinders start to come off. We are uncovering the true state, or uncovering buddha nature. This is important because each day when you sit down, you can recognize that it's a process of gradually uncovering something that's already here. That's why relaxation and letting go are so important. You can't uncover something by harshness or uptightness because those things cover our buddha nature. Stabilizing the mind, bringing out the sharp clarity of mind, needs to be accompanied by relaxation and openness.

You could say that this box we're in doesn't really exist. But from our point of view, there is a box, which is built from all the obstructions, all the habitual patterns and conditioning that we have created in our life. The box feels very, very real to us. But when we begin to see through it, to see past it, this box has less and less power to obstruct us. Our buddha nature is always here, and if we could be relaxed enough and awake enough, we would experience just that.

So trust this gradualness and welcome in a quality of patience and a sense of humor because if the walls came down too fast we wouldn't be ready for it. It would be like a drug trip where you have this mind-blowing experience but then you can't integrate the new way of seeing and understanding into your life.

The path of meditation isn't always a linear path. It's not like you begin to open, and you open more and more and you settle more and more, and then all of a sudden the confining box is gone forever. There are setbacks. I often see with students a kind of "honeymoon period" when they experience a time of great openness and growth in their practice, and then they have a kind of contraction or regression. And this is often terribly frightening or discouraging for many students. A regression in your practice can create crippling doubt and a lot of emotional setback. Students wonder if they've lost their connection to meditation forever because the "honeymoon period" felt so invigorating, so true.

But change happens, even in our practice. This is a fundamental truth. Everything is always changing because it's alive and dynamic. All of us will reach a very interesting point in our practice when we hit the brick wall. It's inevitable. Change is inevitable with relationships, with careers, with anything. I love to talk to people on the meditation path when they're at the point of the brick wall: they think they're ready to quit, but I feel they're just beginning. If they could work with the unpleasantness, the insult to ego, the lack of certainty, then they're getting closer to the fluid, changing, real nature of life.

Hitting the brick wall is just a stage. It means you've reached a point where you're asked to go even further into open acceptance of life as it is, even into the unpleasant feelings of life. The real inspiration comes when you finally join in with that fluidity, that openness. Before, you were cruising with your practice, feeling certain about it, and that feeling can be "the best" in many ways. And then wham! You're given a chance to go further.

26

CREATE A CIRCLE
OF PRACTITIONERS

The clear seeing that tends to develop in meditation practice can lead to genuine compassion because it's through steadfastness with this continual succession of difficult or pleasing circumstances—and with all the moods and personality traits that you see in yourself—that you begin to have some genuine understanding of other people. That's because we're all the same in this way. I may have more aggression than you do, but you may have more craving than I do. I may not know very much about jealousy, but I may know a lot about pride or envy or loneliness, or I may know a lot about feeling unworthy. In some sense, if we just begin to have this emotional honesty with ourselves with what we begin to see about ourselves in meditation, then we begin to realize what other people are up against—just like us. And then we begin to have some compassion for other people.

In Buddhism, there's something called the "three jewels." They are the three most precious supports in your life; they are what you turn toward when you need support or encouragement.

The first jewel is the Buddha, not as someone to lean on and answer all your questions and save you, but as an example of what you also can do. The second is the dharma, the teachings and practices that will help you. And the third is the *sangha,* the community of people who are also committed to awakening.

To me, sangha is a central support in meditation practice. Sangha is a community outside the realm of our work life and our everyday life, a place where we refrain from competition and one-upping each other. It's also an opportunity to put the brakes on people-pleasing behaviors. Rather, we tell each other the truth of our experience.

The image that's usually used for sangha in Buddhist community is an image of everyone standing together and maintaining unconditional friendship. They are not leaning on each other. If someone falls, not everybody falls. At the basis of an enlightened or awakened society, there are individuals who are taking responsibility for their own escalations and spin-offs, their own judgments and prejudices. They are helping each other with kindness and compassion. They give food to those who are hungry, and they give help to those who are sick. By sharing your experiences on the path, you might be helping another person—not from an up-down position, but from friend to friend. And sangha members do not have to live in the same place. You can pen pal with a fellow practitioner, or you talk on the phone. It is hard to go at this practice alone. And participating in a community of practitioners can make a big difference, especially when we hit those bumps in the road when our practice isn't smooth sailing.

27

CULTIVATE A SENSE
OF WONDER

When we look at life, we see that we really don't
know anything for sure. When you travel to for-
eign lands, it's such a good experience because
you realize that people think differently in every single country.
It's particularly good to go to Asian and Third World countries,
where people often think about things from an entirely different vantage point. You realize that most of your assumptions
about reality come from your culture, from the era in which
you were born, from your economic group, from your gender.
There are a lot of assumptions about good and bad that are not
universally held. This is the reason we have wars: one person
has an idea of good that is someone else's idea of bad, and as
a result people kill each other. Throughout the history of the
human race, people have killed each other because they have
different ideas about what's right and good.

The slogan "Regard all dharmas as dreams" encourages us
to begin to wonder about everything. Take trees, for example.

How about really looking at the trees where you live, exploring their bark and their leaves, noticing the way they smell? How about the grass, the air? See if you can go beyond just thinking, "Oh, yes, I know, it's just another boring old spruce tree." Allow yourself to get excited when you see hardwood trees—something with leaves that's getting green because it's spring. Let trees perk you up. Say "yes" to them. Let yourself be filled with wonder when you gaze at them.

I recently read an account of a man, a Native American, who became very sick. He lived in the early part of the twentieth century. He went into a coma, and the way the events turned out, when he came out of this coma he was in the white people's village. (I'm not really sure how he got there, but that's where he was.) And then this very interesting thing happened. In the mythology of his people, there was a long-held belief that said that when you die you go west to the great ocean, and in his people's myths there's a description of going through one tunnel after another to get there. People go through dozens of tunnels, heading west, to the great ocean. And this amazing thing happened to this man. He was taken on a train west, through tunnels, to the ocean. They were taking him to a big city. The story goes on, but the significant thing was that for the rest of his life he thought he was dead, because the reality had totally matched his people's myth about death. And the accounts of this man are what I think comes closest to anything I've ever read of what it meant to be a child of illusion. Because the man thought he was dead, from that point on he was completely present. His mind and heart were completely open. He had the curiosity of a very young child, but at the same time he had the experience of a mature, adult man. He was in a culture that was totally alien to him by all standards, but he showed no signs of letting it throw him. He was completely fascinated by everything because he thought, "This is what happens when you die." The story of this man reminds me of how we take so much of our experience for granted. And part of taking everything for granted is that we fear a lot of our experience. Our fear is based on old, hidden memories, old abuses that happened to us. These old, forgotten, buried things cause us to continually react in unfathomable ways and interpret in curious ways, and always edit our experiences and reactions in strange ways to protect ourselves. We fear a lot of the things that come to us, and we don't even know why.

At the same time, we are very, very drawn to other "things." Sometimes it becomes addictive. Things that represent comfort, things that represent some escape from misery, can become addictions. But it's all happening at this level where we take things for granted and simply react against trees and animals; sounds and memories; smells and tastes; people's faces, bodies, and gestures. We take it for granted that these things are the way they are, and therefore we live in a kind of prison.

So how can we bring wonder into our life in the same way as this Native American man? How can we bring curiosity into our life? The answer begins with the meditation instruction about being gentle and honest. Again, every time you say "thinking," do it with such gentleness, with such honesty. All of that drama, all of that hope and fear, all of that entertainment, and all of that terror—whatever it is that goes along with the story that you've been telling yourself—you can just call it "thinking," and you can say that with heart. Remember: all thoughts could be regarded as dreams. To bring wonder into your life, remember that when you don't know, when you feel shaky because you're not sure what's happening, you don't need to run. You don't need to try to come up with an answer that will make the unknown OK. Train in relaxing. Train in softening. Use your meditation practice. Train in holding your seat with those uncertain, insecure, embarrassed, shaky feelings. This is productive of great well-being.

In fact, the only thing that keeps us from being alive and delighted—or alive and interested with some sense of appetite for our life—is that we have no encouragement to sit still. When we feel tense, when we feel pain, when we feel shaky, we have no encouragement to relax and soften our stomach and our shoulders and our mind and our heart. Anytime you want to make something out of your life, let go. Let go more. Soften. This is how your life becomes workable. This is how your life becomes wonderful. We have the seed of spaciousness and wonder in ourselves. We have the seed of warmth in ourselves. Meditation nourishes and waters these seeds.

There's the space that seems to be out there, like the sky and the ocean and the wind, and there's the space that seems to be inside. We could let the whole thing mix up. We could let the whole thing just dissolve into each other and into one big space. Practice is about allowing a lot of space. It's about learning how to connect with that spaciousness that's inside, and the spaciousness that's outside. It's about learning to relax, soften, and open—to connect with the sense that there's actually a lot of room.

170

28

THE WAY OF THE
BODHISATTVA

From the very beginning of this book, we've been studying something called *bodhichitta*. It's said that the Buddha sat under the *bodhi* tree when he attained enlightenment. The word *bodhi* has a lot of different translations, but it basically means "wide awake." Sometimes it's translated as "enlightened." It means a completely open heart, a completely open mind; it means a heart that never closes down, even in the most difficult and horrendous situations. Bodhichitta communicates a mind that never limits itself with prejudices or biases or dogmatic views that are polarized against someone else's opinions. There is no limit to bodhi, no limit to its fluid and all-embracing openness.

The word *chitta* means "heart" and "mind"; it means both things simultaneously, so we define it as "heart-mind." So you could say that bodhichitta is awakened heart-mind, or enlightened heart-mind, or completely open heart-mind. Chögyam Trungpa Rinpoche had a synonym for bodhichitta: he called it 'soft spot.' He said that we all have this "soft spot"; all living beings have this tenderness. Yet somehow we are born feeling that we need to cover it over and protect it. We live in a world where we think we need to contract and put masks over this part of ourselves that's so tender and soft.

Meditation teaches us to nurture the soft spot, to reopen the heart-mind, to allow love to come and go freely. Dissolving the barriers to the soft spot, dissolving the armor around the soft spot, or dissolving the armor around the heart of bodhichitta (which doesn't ever actually shut down) isn't about finding a final answer, a final solution to life. After all, openness means we always need to be willing to be flexible and make it up as we go along. There is always room to open more.

Another definition of the word *bodhichitta* might be "becoming a completely loving person." If someone says, "What is the purpose of spiritual practice?" I personally feel that the ultimate reason why we practice, why we listen to these teachings, why we try to begin to bring this into every moment of our life, is so that we can become completely loving people. And this is what the world needs.

One of the qualities of bodhichitta is a growing ability to relax with the true nature of reality, which is uncertain and unpredictable. From the average person's point of view, life is fundamentally insecure. But from the point of view of being more and more awake, life no longer feels so insecure. Life is always uncertain, it is always unpredictable, but to say it's insecure no longer holds because we begin to feel settled and comfortable in the uncertainty. Meditation allows us to walk more and more into insecurity until it actually becomes more and more our home ground. Life is just as uncertain and unpredictable as it ever was, but we begin to like surprises. Resistance to change and newness starts to melt.

The nature of reality is completely paradoxical. It is not *like this* or *like that* but we definitely think in opposites or polar views. We concretize with our mind because that's where security comes from; we try to get ground under our feet by saying, "It's like this." Taken to its extreme, this becomes fundamentalism, meaning that you hold to a view and you would go to war for it. It's like *this,* and it is no other way.

To the degree that you relax more into uncertainty and groundlessness, you find your heart opening. Your heart opens to the degree that you can allow difficult situations and step into them. Strangely enough, and I'm sorry to share this with you, you do start to see more and more suffering. In case you think this is a path that leads us someplace where we look like cherubs and have wings and no more pain, on this path, you begin to see that there is suffering in the world, and you see it more and more.

As you become enlightened, you increasingly see how our choices perpetuate suffering. An enlightened person wants to see every one of us get smarter about what escalates suffering, and what de-escalates it. And so this business of stepping more and more into groundlessness, or relaxing with groundlessness, becomes something you wish for everyone. You begin to hear that message.

Meditation is a process of transformation, instead of a process of becoming more and more set in our ways. And, as you know, as we get older it's very common to become increasingly fixed in our habits. But then you do meet people who, for some reason, are becoming more and more flexible and open as they age. Which kind of person do you want to be?

Often the powerful moment on the spiritual journey is the moment when pain is getting very strong, and we feel we've met our edge and there's no way to pretty it up. Usually we think spiritual practice is about getting rid of that moment—but actually, that is the moment from which all the patterns of concretizing, of grasping, of spinning off into all these habits to try to get ground under our feet—they all come out of that moment. So at that very moment, we can do something different. And by doing something different we can liberate ourselves.

In the practice I'm recommending, doing something different means *staying* with that moment. I talked about this in terms of meditation practice, how we must let the thoughts and words go and *feel* whatever is happening. We must change our whole view about pain and difficulty and realize that pain is a prime time for spiritual practice. You might say, "*This* is prime time?!" But it is prime time because at that moment, you can either harden into an old pattern or you can soften and do something different. And often doing something different, as I say, is really just staying.

It's said that great suffering creates or brings great compassion. I've always been struck by this particular phrase because, more commonly, great suffering brings great bitterness, great anger, great wish for revenge, and great hardening. You can seize that moment: you can cherish that moment of pain, and rather than letting it harden you in the habitual way and create great suffering, that moment can create great compassion. Instead of hardening into revenge, you shed a tear, and you start going in the direction of love and kindness—for both yourself and others.

We find the love in ourselves. This is the point. Love is not "out there"; it's not in the relationship, and it's not in having the "right" relationship. It's not our career or our job or our family or our spiritual path. On the other hand, if you begin to connect with the fact that you have this good heart, and that it can be nurtured and woken up, then all of that—career, family, spiritual path, relationships, everything—becomes the means for awakening bodhichitta. Your life is it. There's no other place to practice.